MARGARET MEEK

Information

& Book Learning

THIMBLE PRESS

INFORMATION & BOOK LEARNING
comes from The Thimble Press,
publishers since 1970 of
Signal, the thrice-yearly journal devoted to
books and reading for children and young people,
and other writings on literature and literacy.

Acknowledgement:
The lines from T.S. Eliot's *Choruses from 'The Rock' I*
are quoted from *The Complete Poems and Plays of T.S. Eliot*
Faber & Faber, 1969, page 147

Information & Book Learning

ISBN 0 903355 49 3

First published 1996 by
THE THIMBLE PRESS
Lockwood, Station Road, Woodchester,
Stroud, Glos. GL5 5EQ
phone 01453 87 3716   fax 01453 87 8599

Camera-ready copy produced at
The Thimble Press
Printed in Great Britain
by Short Run Press, Exeter

CONTENTS

Where is the wisdom we have lost in knowledge?
Where is the knowledge we have lost in information?

T S ELIOT, *Choruses from 'The Rock' I*

ONE

Introduction:
A continuing concern

The subject of this set of speculations is how children read to learn. I also consider some of the books designed to instruct them about the world, people and ideas. My subject has links with more general and extended reflections on how children become literate at a time of distinctive social change, when the getting, storing and using of information has something of the force of a new doctrine, especially in relation to children's learning in school and their growth in knowledge and understanding.

To turn the starting-point—a simple wondering about how children learn from modern texts—into something more considered has involved different kinds of effort from a teacher whose commitment to children's reading includes a long acquaintance with children's literature: picture books, poetry, narrative fiction and the critical activities that surround these texts. In contrast, books of information, textbooks, reference books and the like are more usually found in the hands of subject specialists in classrooms where the writ of the English teacher does not run. Except, that is, in primary schools, where learning to read is extended into reading to learn: a transition of distinct importance for the rest of schooling and the concern of all teachers of children under eleven.

Why, then, do I believe as I do, that the time has come to look more seriously at books devised for young learners, books that are seen as different from those written in a 'literary' mode, with different pedigrees and histories, books designed to be learned from, in systematic rather than informal ways, where the contents are arranged for pragmatic purposes of instruction or to promote in their readers definable acts of understanding?

Already you see my dilemma. Despite every rephrasing of these sentences, I have difficulty in avoiding the words commonly used for what I want to interrogate, namely, that in children's development as readers they will encounter two distinct and separable categories of books. The simplified formulation of this division is in the labels 'fiction' and 'non-fiction'. The latter are thought of as books offering readers representations of the 'actual' world from which that world can be learned about. The former is the category of stories, novels, which are for pleasure, recreational reading and informal learning.

I suspect that no one reading this believes that the literary convention of dividing books into these two categories is either predictable or absolute. (Where do you put poetry?) But, as it stands, the classification sustains other assumptions about reading and learning. So I begin by declaring that notions of fiction and non-fiction (the pleasurable and the serious) are neither useful nor helpful, tenable even, in contemporary children's learning. Even before they can read, children discover a world full of representations, signs and pictures, so they are not likely to expect texts for learning to be only in books. Moreover, many adults will suggest to them that for knowing about the world, books are a thing of the past. This is not a belief I share. But to argue, as I am about to, that books are important for children's learning is not simply to assume that the books we have are all we need. The opposite is the case.

The first part of my argument begins with a consideration of information, and how the 'getting' of it sits within the distinctive nature of reading as experience. The proposal is partly driven by my conviction that the contents of so-called non-fiction books are offered to children as incontrovertible, authoritative *facts*, which are implicitly assumed to create a picture and an explanation of the world 'as it is'. Since no serious critical activity, such as accompanies traditional children's literature, exists in relation to information books, it therefore seems useful to examine the nature and contents of some conventional books used in school, or read elsewhere, and the recent changes in their contents and production. In so doing it may be possible to discover how young readers are introduced to their cultural history and to current understandings of the societies in which they are growing up. This sequent of the argument also challenges the notion that the discourse of information texts should be, essentially, non-narrative.

The second part considers some individual books in selected subjects so as to examine what is involved in reading them. A fairly general, but unexamined, assumption is that books for learning are necessarily taxing or difficult, and that the effort to read them is somehow part of the discipline of study. An alternative view is that really expert presentation of ideas, and the information they generate, engages the imagination of learners, that a desire to know helps to create more sustained learning in children and more critical reading of information books by teachers, parents and others.

The third part brings together some reconsiderations of the nature and use of information books, and discusses ways in which a more critical climate for considering 'the world as it is' as portrayed for children reading to learn can be achieved.

From time to time during the compilation of these pages I was obliged to reflect on my own inadequacies as someone learning to read subject matter of which I had little previous understanding and even less experience, a condition I now believe I share with many children. Like most confident readers I have always taken the instrumental nature of reading, its usefulness, for granted. To observe how I used books for learning I chose one outside my usual domain, *The Great Wine Blight* by George Ordish, to see how I tackled the details of the spread of phylloxera in the middle of the last century. Imagine, every vine was threatened with extinction. The search for the cause and the cure of this pest is one of the great detective stories of science, not least because the most knowledgeable investigators first mistook the effect of the disease for its cause.

As I had made up my mind to read every page, to engage with the specialized vocabularies of botany, economics, history, as these occurred, and to make sense of scientific inquiry reported in tables, pictures and diagrams, I found I also needed new ways to describe what I was doing and how I read. When I was most at ease, reading from line to line, I recognized the linear textual formation we teach children as the normal way to make meaning from print. At other times, in looking at tables, schedules of costs represented as figures, drawings and sketches, I had to move back and forth to these to find subsidiary clues for demonstrations of what I was reading about in paragraphs composed of sentences. I was also bringing to the reading all I already knew about viticulture from my frequent visits to Burgundy. Confidence in my ability to manage this *radial* movement through unfamiliar subject matters and unfamiliar texts increased as I made a synthesis (not always exact, complete or correct) of the hitherto known and the new details. I had no illusions that I was now an expert on the phylloxera, but I knew that I could ask my Burgundian friends about it and understand their explanations.

As I moved between my own reading to learn and that of children in school, I rediscovered some obvious things. Children get much of the information they want from moving about in the world and asking questions. When they meet book presentation of what they have already encountered, they check out the details, confirming some earlier learning and extending some new insights. Teachers encourage both informal and formal writing about a range of new topics. Gradually school writing and school book learning move closer together in anticipation of the routines of examinations. There are difficulties and discontinuities, some misunderstandings and loss of confidence if too much or too little is expected. (The learners' perception of this is boredom.) But, in the later stages of study, book learning is rewarded if the learner has mastered the formal writing practice of what has been understood. Whether it is imperative formally to teach the discourse of a subject in the early stages of learning its content is a recurrent discussion among educators.

Behind all the details of school and book learning lie the originating *ideas* of those who have contributed to what is known. These ideas generate information when they are put to the test and are seen to make a difference. Think of all the children who learn about the Industrial Revolution and its consequences. How do details they learn influence their view of the present? The essential move in learning is to transform information to understanding. But many books for the young fail to help them to take this step. I said this once before, so I went back to my earlier considerations of information books to see what had changed.

In 1977, when topic books for use in school began to arrive for review in ever-increasing numbers (I was Reviews Editor for *The School Librarian* at the time), I wrote an article for my journal entitled 'What is a horse?'. In it I was fairly scathing about the form and content of most of the books which made up the stock in school libraries, the texts that pupils used for 'projects' or to answer questions on the newly popular worksheets, devised by teachers to deal with the complications of 'mixed ability groups' and the new cross-curricular subjects, such as humanities.

My main criticisms of the new sets of 'non-fiction' were of perplexing, badly written and inaccurate texts, and of the implicit assumption that if the books proved difficult to read, the fault lay always with the readers' lack of skill. Many of the writers had little concern, or so it seemed, to help the readers to come to terms with the information given, and the over-generalized statements were aimed at too wide an audience, or contained some dubious 'facts'. I suggested that the lack of informed criticism of these books and the general ignorance of their relation to what was expected to count as school learning in a changing world were serious matters. Although I knew that books have always been, primarily, an economic commodity for trade and that books for schools are a safe market, I accused topic-book publishers of deliberately playing that market.

These complaints have been repeated since then by others, and extended by Eleanor von Schweinitz, who declares that 'overall the picture is rather a dispiriting one' (*Books for Keeps*, March 1989, 8). I think that the general scene has brightened since then, but the existence of current detailed programmes of study for use in schools makes publishers only too keen to give teachers what they say they want, a relief from responsibility for so many topics, without further consideration of the learners.

Over the years many of these issues have returned to perplex me. Despite all that has been written about reading and understanding, the notion that knowledge has an objective existence, that it can be transmitted, either in parts or whole and entire, to a range of individual minds where it will remain in memory until called upon is still prevalent, not only in schools. There has grown up a concomitant conviction that knowledge, in its written form as 'subject matter' or as 'information', is now so important for our variegated modern styles of living that everyone who wants to study is expected to learn how to *access* (now a verb) it. The growth of the study of studying, apart from what has to be studied and why, has accelerated.

I have also pondered a distinction I now think is important: between *being* interested and *becoming* interested. Young people discover that certain topics, especially those associated with the fervour of collection, are considered by adults to be their interests: football club stickers, stamps, the latest craze in computer games or

11

the 'mini-figs' of war games and imaginary battles. These are social and 'club' fashions. Often they are temporary although some develop into more sustained learning. Train spotters become train drivers; war-games players develop an interest in military history. Becoming interested in a more prolonged sense is a gradual realization that some discovery learning is worth pursuing beyond its immediate modishness. It commands a different kind of adherence; it becomes the kind of study which helps the learner to tolerate the *longueurs* which are part of gaining any skill or understanding, especially when the mastery of craft or knowledge is an object of desire. Learning to read a challenging book really well is an example.

For someone who has spent a long time thinking about the reflexive processes of comprehension, this increased emphasis on study as a set of isolable, decontextualized 'skills', most of which are related to the new technologies for storing information, created additional problems about reading and understanding. Reading for information—book learning especially, as I practise it—is about thinking, wondering, and sometimes understanding, with the ever-present possibility of being unsettled.

The notion that information has to be *retrieved* has grown up with the development of computers and is fed back to its older source, the use of books for reference. In recent dictionary entries, 'retrieve' now means 'make newly available'. Earlier uses are 'to bring back', 'rediscover', 'set right'. Today information, however we may decide to define or describe it, is seen as lurking, stored, in files of different kinds in ever more sophisticated systems, some of it, we are told, illegally. It has to be 'flushed out', as the older dictionaries say, by those who know how the machines work and how the contents are 'keyed'.

The real problem is an intellectual not a practical one. How many and what kinds of understanding do pupils need to be able to use for their specific kinds of inquiry, school-based or privately initiated? We cannot issue a list for everyone. Are the 'skills' that students must acquire expected to last longer than the systems they unlock? Experience suggests that information is best learned in practice where the study is deemed by pupils or their teachers to be important, for only then will the acquired information be seen as valuable.

The more I think about it, the more I am persuaded that young people who leave school as early as they can, or who have been deflected from study by its association with the boring and unprofitable reading of books, will not be induced to continue their education by the promise of greater contact with more sophisticated information-retrieval procedures, nor by the notion that old school boredom will be dispelled by more exciting machines. The problem remains: how are we to help young learners to understand the nature of knowing in those areas of the curriculum where their curiosity, their imagination, interests and energies can be both engaged and sustained? In a literate society crammed with print many school leavers have unused competences, and a particular kind of powerlessness, because they have not been encouraged to see that they can *produce* consequential information from their own ideas and experience.

When we read in order to understand something more, or more clearly, about the world, the result is not a straightforward addition to the store of information we believe we already possess. Instead it is an increase in our confidence that we have sorted something out: a belief that we can cope with another thing we have to do, or that we possess a better understanding of the world as a whole and our life in it. We began this sorting out when we were quite young. We see children doing it all the time, especially when they begin to read. Their world is different. We can't do their thinking for them. But we can take a look at their coming to know, their learning from the books we give them and the texts they choose for themselves, to see if these are really as helpful as they might be.

What follows is a sketch of a much bigger inquiry. Because my learning in certain subjects (science is the glaring example) is scant, I make no claim to have solved the problems I draw attention to. My concern is to suggest that *book* learning, for all its ubiquity in schools and elsewhere, has never been really carefully investigated, that is, carefully observed and reported on in the context of children's coming to know and understand. Scholars, the acknowledgedly successful learners, have other plans; teachers are bound by didactic obligations. Children are rarely asked well enough to tell us how they learn. So I suggest that the subject of how books teach or help children to learn is still wide open.

TWO

Information: Literacy as praxis or the world in bits

A pressing problem about information as currently encountered is not how to get it, but what to do with it or how to ignore it when it comes in forms we neither want nor need, like junk mail. How do we know how to judge the nature and importance of what we are told or invited to read in the print all around us? Most teachers know the classroom legend of the eight-year-old who wrote in a reading diary: 'I have read a book about dogs. It told me more than I want to know.'

Our cultural preoccupation with information is the result of changes in systems of communication and record-keeping. Our dilemma is not how to define or describe information, but how to set into some kind of order the vast quantities we amass of it, and to think about these huge computer collections of items—the world in bits—in relation to human knowing and understanding.

Information is recognizable as news—a definition that dictionaries trace back to 1450. A single new item, fact, letter, story, statement may change our view of things: the roses are out, the West Indians are batting, there is a chance of peace in the Middle East. Each informative event makes a change in our consciousness or mental context if we pay more than passing attention to it. Something we see on the late-night news is part of our mental set the next morning. Every day we reinform ourselves, by glancing at a newspaper for the time of a film, reading a recipe or the dosage on a medicine bottle, planning the quickest way to a destination, and thousands of similar actions. To dispel our ignorance we ask someone who is better informed than we are, or we perform the common social habits that let us find telephone numbers, how much salt for the fish, what the pound is worth.

We use our literacy as praxis, to do things: we look for information in printed sources because we have learned to read and write, as part of our being at home in our society. Answers to our everyday questions are netted in our cultural habits of talking, listening, reading and writing. 'Bits' of information add to, and change, what we already know. If this does not happen, we simply let them slip away beyond recall.

To understand what counts as information we have to see it in relation to our view of the world. As 'data', information appears to be an impersonal collection of records, the given, available for processing, linking or retrieval as *facts*. Nothing is so incontrovertible as this word suggests. Information is never neutral, unless, perhaps, when it is encoded as mathematics. All written records come with the world view of the writer and the socially acknowledged authority of the experts who compiled them. The tradition of holding authors responsible for what they write in books is well embedded in our culture.

In contrast, compilers of databanks and makers of databases are less well identified. Those who plan computer programs are protected from theft; they also set the conditions of others' access, the kinds of questions that can be asked and the nature of the answers. So when we are confronted with what a computer tells us is 'the given' in the information we 'retrieve', we need to encourage ourselves and our children to ask 'who says?' and 'who sees?'. Good readers learn to do this as they grow in skill and confidence, usually with teaching help and encouragement. Getting information is never simply collecting bits; it is part of the praxis of critical literacy.

By itself, information is neither experience nor knowledge. Discovering what we need to know may be a short-term process, like reading the little screen to find out how much money we have in the bank. If we want to understand how this banking system works and the capitalist economy that sustains it, we have to contemplate a more prolonged engagement with accountancy. In both cases, what we come to know informs, changes our awareness.

Here is the most quoted sentence in the Bullock Report, *A Language for Life*. It reminds us now, as aptly as it did in 1975, that if information is to be of more than temporary significance to us, 'What is known must be brought to life afresh in the mind of every knower. To bring knowledge into being is a formulating process and language is its ordinary means, whether in speaking or writing, or in our inner monologues of thought.' (50, 4.9)

15

Children encounter information in abundance before they know how to sort it out in order to make their world a recognizable place. When they go to school they are taught, directly or indirectly, ways of linking their experience into patterns of learning; sand and water play becomes floating and sinking, spelling has rules and exceptions, multiplication tables have a repetitious rhythm. Learning 'by heart' to train the memory has never ceased to be part of schooled instruction in the acquisition of useful knowledge. Growing older, children discover the formulating processes for themselves, especially when they notice that the books they read provide ways of expressing what they learn. They begin to transform information into understanding, something no book or machine can do for them. As they are human learners, their imagination of how things *might* be takes them beyond the information given. To qualify as a knower, every novice has to learn how to be at ease with the conventions of texts, how they are composed, designed and written in order to be read. The written ordering of a subject is its *discourse*, a word that still means talking about something.

Information retrieval is rarely a form of free-ranging inquiry. In much current writing on this topic, the seeker is expected to have a 'need' to find something 'out', although 'browsing' is usually encouraged, whether in books or on screens. Even before we begin the search process we confront questions of what we are encouraging children to do, both about how they are to get information and about what they will then do with it. Are we asking them to find out what we could tell them? Whose questions are they answering? How do we know the best starting place for their inquiries? Or are we simply offering school pupils the opportunity to practise what are called *skills*, in a generic or generalized fashion, so that when they have something to look 'up' they will apply the taught routines, irrespective of the subject matter? Are we separating information-getting from learning? At the back of my mind is the question that Herbert Spencer asked a century ago when he queried the contents of the curriculum in public schooling: 'What knowledge is of most worth?'

When we think of young people leaving school at sixteen or eighteen with the intention of living independent lives, and the ever-increasing documentation that surrounds even the most straightforward transactions with public authorities, we can understand the impulse that lay behind the 'Need To Know' project in a school in London's South Hackney in the late 1970s. Teachers and librarians wanted to help school-leavers to understand the workings of civic bureaucracy. At the time, the argument that the transmitted experience of friends and neighbours 'was no longer enough' seemed a sensible one. So pupils were given practice in 'simple searching skills' in the library, at the Citizens' Advice Bureau, and in reading a booklet of local information.

With hindsight, the researchers' discoveries might seem to have been predictable. First, it isn't possible to define the needs of others, even with the reasonable-seeming question 'What do you want to know?' Second, the 'common networks of friends and neighbours' proved to be more secure and helpful than the researchers thought they were. One of the inquiry tasks the pupils were set was to find out from public documents the date on which they could legally leave school. Everyone knew it already.

The Hackney project, and others like it, handed down the conviction that information and study skills should be introduced as part of all teaching across the range of curriculum subjects. The rationale, that good study habits should be acquired when children move from learning to read to reading to learn, became generally agreed by those who advised teachers in school. Formal instruction in information skills was devised in the wake of research carried out by Lunzer and Gardner for the Schools Council in 1979. They said that children's reading for information could be enhanced by appropriate reading 'strategies', such as SQ3R (Survey, Question, Read, Recite, Review), first proposed by F.P. Robinson in 1946. This procedure, they said, 'can and should be applied to every text when reading is undertaken for the purposes of learning'. The teachers who conscientiously put these operations into practice complained they were too cumbersome and unnecessarily repetitive. A revised form of the Lunzer and Gardner proposals, DARTS (Directed Activities Related to Texts), is generally promoted in classes where talk is seen as contributing significantly to children's learning, especially when they are being encouraged to move from a literal reading of a text to shared meanings. Although few teachers try to insist on 'directed activities' with all reading for learning, there is no doubt that, especially in secondary schools, pupils should come to understand the *constructedness* of writing.

In a literate society, people discover different ways of finding things out from written sources, including asking those who already have experiences of what common documents contain. No matter how insistent their teachers are about 'looking up', learners adopt routines that suit them. Think of how young children quickly learn how to find out what is on television and how to read written instructions for toys and tools they want to make work. I'm not sure that their reading to learn from unfamiliar books will improve by following directions about reading if they have no awakened interest in the topic. The word 'tackle' (as in football?) appears regularly in books about helping children to read what adults suppose is difficult. Do you think the contents of a book have to be reorganized before children can learn from them? Let me show you why I think the choice of emphasis on what children should learn to do in order to read to learn is a crucial decision in matters related to book learning.

In a paper called 'Teaching Information Skills in the Primary School' David Wray offers an 'integrated approach' by means of 'suitable skill development activities' to help teachers to 'make project work meaningful'. The italics in the passage are mine.

Wray suggests that the process of *using* information seems to include six main stages: *defining* the subject and purpose; *locating* the information (the list of places includes not only libraries, books, other texts and people, but also all modern electronic storage systems); *selecting* information; *organizing* information; *evaluating* information and *communicating* the results. To encourage these 'uses', teachers are to devise aims, make plans, implement plans, evaluate progress and instruct pupils how to do these things. Books are to be organized in classrooms and their system of classification explained to the children.

In a later article Wray goes further. He wants schoolbooks of information to be written in the way children have been specially taught to read them. That is, the teachers teach the children to read what they have taught the writers to write. This hoop-snake view of learning from books is reading *management*, derived from a positivistic view of knowledge as a kind of naive realism. Within it, the teacher's view of learning and the learner's view of knowing become of less importance than instructions about how the text is to be 'tackled'.

Here now is a different picture. It depends on a conception of information that includes uncertainty, probability, hypothesis making, using information in the puzzling-out mode. It starts from the assumption that no information exists as purely detachable fact, despite its heuristic helping-to-learn function. Informative teaching and learning in this mode demand interpersonal dialogue, whether in the silence of reading and writing or in the exchanges of classroom discussions. Meet Jerome Bruner's teacher.

> I recall a teacher, her name was Miss Orcutt, who made the statement in class, 'It is a very puzzling thing not that water turns to ice at 32 degrees Fahrenheit, but that it should change from a liquid into a solid'. She then went on to give us an intuitive account of Brownian movement and of molecules, expressing a sense of wonder that matched, indeed bettered, the sense of wonder I felt at that age (around ten) about everything I turned my mind to, including at the far reach such matters as light from extinguished stars still traveling toward us though their sources had been snuffed out. In effect, she was inviting me to extend *my* world of wonder to encompass *hers*. She was not just *informing* me. She was, rather, negotiating the world of wonder and possibility. Molecules, solids, liquids movement were not facts; they were to be used in pondering and imagining. Miss Orcutt was the rarity. She was a human event, not a transmission device. (*Actual Minds, Possible Worlds*, 126)

Miss Orcutt chose her examples for their 'amenableness to imaginative transformation'. She invites speculation so that her pupils are to become part of the shared and sharing thinking which not only gives them access to knowledge but also lets them create and interpret it because it has come alive for them. They are not just using information. They are learning to learn.

These ideas of Bruner's show me how the increased emphasis on the management of information skills has created something akin to a second-stage reading scheme. The explicitness of David Wray's operations, his designed learning to help inexperienced readers who are not familiar with information sources and 'handling' print, obliterates the wonder, the speculation, and replaces it with the exactness of exercises. The implication is that the pupils Wray has in mind cannot be encouraged to speculate because they need help in defining what they want to know and how to go about finding out. My belief is that inexperienced readers reject 'looking up' as boring because it takes so long and is rarely fuelled by desire and wonder. The result is that these pupils are even less inclined to look for information in books as a matter of habit because for them book learning is a series of 'steps to strategies'. Bruner calls this the 'flat declaration of fixed facticity'.

In contrast, Miss Orcutt behaves like a scientist, practising curiosity. She also encourages negotiation and sharing in ways that remind me of reading classes where the learners not only get the words right but also treat their interactions with the book text as a human event, one that touches them, informs them and transforms their notion of what learning can be like.

The second reason for my finding an ally in Miss Orcutt is that she counts on what the children have already shown they can do when they are thinking. At the age of ten they will have become confident enough in reading and writing to operate certain literate competences without needing to pay attention to them. The ten-year-olds I know can read all the signs in their environment, including TV commercials, without others having to explain to them how to do these things.

The literacy teaching that goes on in most successful classrooms makes the particulars of reading operations disappear into the efficiency of their use. If 'information strategies' are constantly given attention they become ends in themselves, a task to be done with arms folded at the end of it, when what has been discovered should be the means to other ends. The 'purposes of study' are the reasons children give themselves for paying attention to what they are expected to learn. They are not always the teachers' purposes; these are often inadequately explained. In the end, it is the pupils' desire to learn that takes them beyond the information given.

If we are to understand book learning, we must look at its social aspects beyond the boundaries of the classroom, even when most of the books children are expected to read are located there. I find it difficult to believe that the *skill* of getting information is divisible into discrete operations. Like comprehension and understanding, it is a unitary not a multiple activity, in no way different from the other purposive uses of literacy in the context of learning.

You may retort, with good reason, that I haven't learned well enough to read for information. It is true that, having tried them all at different times in my teaching, I now circumvent many of the repetitive activities that study experts say I should perform. My attempts to carry out the recommendations in David Wray's list, especially the one about specifying as clearly as possible what I want to find out, have made me sceptical.

Because I know there are pitfalls in being 'quite precise' about what I want to discover, I rarely insist on absolute certainty that I know what I want to find out before I take a book in hand. When I need to find out the weight of a letter for the post, the date of a meeting, I know that exactness counts, as it also does when looking for a library book or a word in the dictionary. But these bits of information do not need informed or informing reading. They are examples of ordinary literacy as praxis. In what now follows the distinction is important.

THREE

Narrative: Facts and non-fiction fallacies

Storytelling is something we all do and understand. The habit is so deeply sunk in us, historically and culturally, that we recognize our common humanity in all the tales we tell and hear, from childhood to old age, waking and dreaming.

Why do we tell stories? Your own answer to this question is the one you will believe. My conviction is that we would die if we didn't, not least because stories make it possible for us to imagine that there is a time called the present between what we remember of the past and what we think might happen in the future. Stories let us make our lives into a coherent whole alongside the lives of others, turning our experience into learning. Before they can do any of this reflecting, children use the stories they hear as a kind of memory, and they tell themselves what the world might be like in the time to come.

The famous storyteller Ursula Le Guin once asked this question at a gathering of experts who were discussing narrative, the word we use to cover all kinds of 'storying'. Her answer was, we tell stories 'because we are so organized as to take actions that prevent our dissolution into the surroundings', that is, to distinguish ourselves as who and what we are. She continues,

I know a very short story which might illustrate this hypothesis. You will find it carved into a stone about three feet up from the floor of the north transept of Carlisle Cathedral in the north of England ... It was carved in runes, one line of runes, laboriously carved into the stone. A translation into English is posted up nearby in typescript under glass. Here is the whole story:

Tolfink carved these runes in this stone.

... It doesn't have much beginning or end. The material was obdurate, and life is short. Yet I would say Tolfink was a reliable narrator. Tolfink bore witness at least to the existence of Tolfink, a human being unwilling to dissolve entirely into his surroundings. (94)

Neither Ursula Le Guin's explanation nor mine has any attraction for naive realists. They reject the idea that narration is a proper way to write what has to be learned as school lessons. Instead, they insist that books of information must show readers the world 'as it is', in terms that match children's ability to understand it. Thus, if they are to acquire knowledge, pupils have to leave behind accounts of the world that are fiction or individual experiences and learn the formal language of books. So when 'the seaside' comes into lessons, warm recollections of summer holidays have to be turned into book sentences about the sun, sand and tides. Secondary school pupils put the starfish they find into a category of marine biology.

In accordance with this view, when information is written as narrative, the story distracts the reader from the 'facts'. One commentator goes so far as to say the narrative needs only one reading strategy; children should learn 'flexible' strategies. She is convinced that there is 'less material to absorb' in narratives, whereas there is 'much material to absorb' in non-narratives (Neate, 1992). You must judge for yourself. My reading does not uphold these claims.

The teacher's book of Ginn Science Information Books, designed for children in the early years of primary school and published in 1991, was emphatic that:

There are currently few books which make scientific information accessible to the youngest children in the appropriate form. Many existing titles mingle fact and fiction in the belief that making science into a 'story' makes it more approachable and entertaining. However, our opinion is that it can be confusing to mix fact and fantasy. This approach is not used in science books for older children and adults, and the confusion of forms may mislead early readers about the purposes for which they are reading. Presented in the correct way, at an appropriate level, scientific information is interesting in its own right and the child will be motivated to read on by the pleasures of acquiring new knowledge, studying beautiful photographs and interpreting simple diagrams.

This quotation exposes a number of common fallacies: that there is one correct way to write about science, that narratives are always stories and that stories are always fictive, or, as the writer says, 'fantasy', with an emphasis on the readers' enjoyment rather than on their learning. More important, the statements contain the old-fashioned idea that all fiction is untrue, therefore 'unscientific'.

Parents who want to wean their reading children on to factual matters as soon as possible look for texts which begin, 'This is a tent' or 'Here is a tractor', convinced that progress in reading means moving on from stories. I have yet to find a way to dispel in adults the belief that we begin by believing fairy stories and grow up when we tell ourselves the truth. What worries people about storying? The only way I know to sort out the puzzle is to demonstrate that stories nest in every kind of text, especially in the running narrative in our heads where we explain things to ourselves.

Children learn to read when their world, with its pictures and signs, and their curiosity about books and writing impel them to. The attentiveness they give to reading in the early stages is both intense and complex. Until they are fluent and confident about reading aloud they are concerned to balance the exactness of getting the words right (to please adults) with the fluency of getting the meaning of the text (to please themselves). When they can orchestrate their knowledge of print and their experience of language in the world, they concentrate on the meaning of what they read. Good readers are certain that they do not look at one word at a time. Instead, they discover in books both the world they inhabit and the other world that the writers and artists make for them. A story like Shirley Hughes's *Alfie Gets in First*, about a little boy who finds he is locked into his house with the catch of the front door just out of his reach and his mother and baby sister outside, shows the reader that, while all the people in the street are trying to help, Alfie is able to solve the problem for himself.

Where but in a book can young readers see both sides of the predicament at once long enough to understand both points of view? This is distinctive book learning: the beginning of contemplation.

A single instance gives only a glimpse of the great leap that children make in the direction we call forward when they come to learn from the written word. It happens quite early. There is no step-by-step way through the world of facts. Instead, readers tune in to new voices telling them things in different kinds of language. They remember what they read because they are delighted to learn book words from all kinds of texts, narrative or non-narrative. Here is Paddy Clarke doing it in Roddy Doyle's autobiographical novel:

> The real name for soccer was association football. Association football was played with a round ball on a rectangular pitch by two sides of eleven people. The object is to score goals, i.e. force the ball into the opponents' goal, which is formed by two upright posts upon which is mounted a crossbar. I learned this off by heart. I liked it. It didn't sound like rules; it sounded cheeky. (53)

I suspect we all have some of this kind of learning in our personal histories. Children do not need to distinguish categories of fiction and non-fiction. They find facts in both. But they discover early that some books are designed to teach them things, probably because, when these books are read aloud, the instructive tone sounds like lessons. Before long, a growing interest in a particular subject encourages them to remember which books tell them what they want to know or to remember. Charles Darwin was not yet in his teens when he wrote in his autobiography, 'From reading White's *Selborne* I took much pleasure in watching the habits of birds, and even made notes on the subject.' Despite his later fame, his early experience is not unique. Many children know how to make a 'garden calendar'.

For young learners, the shape of a story, the linking of the beginning and the end, creates a reading act. To make this happen, the reader keeps going, and thus finds out that reading is a powerful thing to be able to do. Adults congratulate them. The best books for children entice them to find out more about what reading can be like. They see how the events fit with what they know, and learn to discuss what they think and feel about what happens. In talking about the adventures of Alfie, the children I listened to suggested to each other what they might have done in a similar situation. They were 'going beyond' what they had read so that they made the book experiences their own. More evidence of this kind of reading is in a video called *Creating a Community of Readers*, which shows children discussing Anthony Browne's picture book, *Gorilla*, in this way. To onlookers this all seems very straightforward, but the implications are worth considering.

We know that, almost as soon as they are read to for the first time, the language of books begins to appear in children's speech, especially when they link book incidents and everyday events. We are less informed about how children take their experience of texts into the world. Yet many a child on a first visit to a zoo has recognized a giraffe and said its name aloud, as the result of first having seen the picture of one in a book. Many children quickly build up a topic interest from reading before they have seen the 'real thing'. Book learning is both life-to-text and text-to-life. The evidence for this is clearer in beginners than in adolescents because the incidents are more striking. But we also recognize the beginnings of new learning in teenagers who deliberately use the special vocabularies of subjects in which they want to become experts. They not only learn chemistry or economics; they lay claim to these by a deliberate parade of the formal language. Different ways of putting the world and books together seem to bear out Frank Smith's assertion that 'we learn the worlds we create' (47).

Here is my great friend, Josh Hook, at age five, already a practised storyteller as the result of having been read to, putting together what he has learned about the Vikings from book texts and *Blue Peter* on television. This comes from the tape recording his mother made of his explanation. She tries to help him and can't always decipher some things he doesn't say clearly. The hesitations are an important point in his thinking; he is summoning the next bit of his understanding as he tries to sort out how to make a telling of it all. He leaves out words that a writer would have to put in. The italics are Josh's emphases.

There was knights in armour—no I don't want to say that—Vikings came from Scandinavia—all the people were afraid of the Vikings—they stole their treasure and sailed away. er, er, At *home* Vikings used—um—small boats called fishing boats—and the big boats were called longboats—uh— to do *farming*— um—um they had all sorts of things.—*And*— but for fighting they had hatchets, weapons—and shields. er-er-er-This is—what was that things again? (Adult, WHICH THING?) These jewellery things. Those jewellery things what—(BROOCHES?) Yea—and buckles to fasten their clothes and a—and er—Talked of fighting a dragon (Tape unclear, could be Thor) Odin on a horse with eight legs—and you can try making a Viking boat—cut out cardboard and stick it together and that's the end.

Josh wants to make this into a story, but he knows that the

details have a different kind of verity. As he speaks, he sorts out Vikings from knights in armour. Both topics are book business; neither is part of his everyday knowing. His mother remembers what lies behind this version: Alison Uttley's *Fuzzypeg* and a book from the Macdonald Starter series (*Vikings* by C. Oram, 1972). Josh is also recalling his visit to a castle, which has to be bypassed because it is not part of the Viking saga; it belongs to the knight's tale. Television has added the relevant details about weapons and boats. He knows that words like *jewellery* have a collective function. Here there is no distinction between fiction and non-fiction in the source material Josh is dealing with. His main concern is to perform his knowing, so we see how many kinds of experience of texts, books and pictures help him to create the reality he now gives to the Vikings.

It is not an accident that this example is from a boy. Parents are inclined to believe that boys need or are specially drawn to factual representations in ways that let them read shorter passages more often than longer books. This is sometimes offered as an explanation of why boys move less quickly than girls into sustained reading. Boys are also confirmed in their reading about activities and 'the way things work' by playing computer games they share and discuss with their peers. The social conformities that emphasize perceived difference in preferences then become part of gender stereotyping. The result *may* be that boys read less continuous text than girls. But if this is the case, it is also true that girls are not encouraged enough to explore different kinds of information texts.

There is no doubt that, as they encounter writing in the world of school, children will be expected to learn and to follow certain conventions. It is equally certain that these conventions are no more than temporary; writing changes. We saw Josh discovering how to tell stories that let him explain his understanding of book texts to himself and others. Here are sentences from more of his stories which show he is highly aware of different kinds of discourse. He is pretending to read a news bulletin and a weather forecast like those he has heard:

'Mr Whitelaw said that all the rates of Thatcher's money must be given to Carol Fox.'

'Somewhere in Australia a hundred bargains has been cut off by Thatcher.'

'There will be more rain and cloud in the west of Greenland.'

Josh's mother, Carol Fox, says: 'The knowledge slips into the stories spontaneously, reflecting an unconscious awareness of the way stories persuade us of the reality of new and invented worlds.' Later, Josh will discover he can have a conscious grasp of what is already familiar to him.

In the first instance, non-narrative discourses come to children not from books but in literacy as praxis. In Josh's case it is in the 'sounded writing' of television. He has discovered that in different programmes the subject matter has different words and 'tunes'. Already he knows how to express explanations, answers, hypotheses and plans when his storytelling role demands these. As children learn more about the world it does not seem strange to them that there should be many ways in language for identifying differences of subject matter. Narrative has already taught them that this is what happens. Our first concern, therefore, is not to show them the words but to engage them in the thinking that the topic provokes. Children's storytelling has its own logic which should not be written off as inconsequential. Many people refuse to see that it is a way to conscious reflexive thinking.

This brings me back to my concern about information books devised as lessons. Before children go to school there is no division in their view of the world as fiction and non-fiction, imagination and fact. Some like books about tractors better than books of stories, but this is often over-generalized. We underestimate the complexity of children's narrative understanding when we give them simplified fact books. What we need is not more books to teach them how to write in different generic modes but much more observation of how children stretch their language to match and to explore their experience of both books and the world.

In this connection the complex role of imagination in childhood is discounted too early, especially in its relation to the understanding of facts in the sorting out children do in order to come to terms with social living. Explaining the influences which made him a poet, W.H. Auden recounts that his early reading texts were books of geology. He read them with a particular kind of attention between the ages of six and twelve, that is, the length of the time span of primary schooling. I have quoted this in other places to make this point. Here I repeat it because it has a special relevance to this argument as a whole. Auden tells us:

> Between the ages of six and twelve I spent a great many of my waking
> hours constructing a private sacred world, the principal elements of
> which were two: a limestone landscape based on the Pennine moors in
> the North of England, and an industry: lead-mining. It was, unlike a
> poem, a pure private world of which I was the only human inhabitant. I
> had no wish to share it with others, nor could I have done so. However, I
> needed the help of others in procuring the *raw materials for its construc-*
> *tion* [italics added]. Others, principally my parents, had to provide me
> with maps, guide books, textbooks on geology and mining machinery,
> and when the occasion offered, take me down real mines. Since it was a
> purely private world, theoretically, I suppose, I should have been free to
> imagine anything I liked, but in practice I found it was not so. I felt in-
> stinctively that I was bound to obey certain rules. I could choose, for
> example, between two winding-engines, but they had to be real ones I
> could find in my books; I was not free to invent one. I could choose
> whether a mine should be drained by a pump or an adit, but magical ones
> were forbidden. (584-5)

Perhaps because I believe that poets are truly representative
human beings and not special cases, I think this is as good an explanation as we shall find of how the young can be encouraged to
enter the world of book learning; if, that is, we discover how to let
them know that their interests can be widened and diversified by
'all kinds of writing', and that we are not repressive about the texts
they choose for themselves. However, I think it is also time we had
more exact examples and better research models of how children
turn information into understanding. It is clear that, without the
transforming force of the imagination, what we are told to regard
as facts have no combinatorial power, whether in chronological or
non-chronological forms, as logic or anything else. My contention
is that the hypothesis-making habit of the scientist begins with the
'what if' of the fairy tale.

This means that children should come to know and to experience just how wide is the range of choice in book learning, and that
their parents and teachers should know how versatile, inventive,
powerful and universal are the ways of narrative, stories and storytelling in all our lives. Before we approach the topic books, however, we must consider what is involved in 'looking up', a habit
that is expected to last long after school.

29

FOUR

The Quick Fix: Reference books

Most of us use familiar sources of information in domestic settings when we need to. The slickest users of the telephone directory are those who make most calls: a skill the young acquire early. In ordinary circumstances children see adults 'looking up' in calendars, address books, timetables, street maps, cookery books and notices for local and other events. Emergencies or special inquiries produce the Yellow Pages. Families stick notes on walls where the address and phone number of the doctor can be seen quickly. The distinguishing feature of this kind of search is the need to know *now*. Any interruption of the process, any distraction or false trail and the search goes cold. The search for the quick fix of information is something we do in order to have done with it as soon as possible.

Behind a great deal of looking up, especially from printed sources, is the principle of alphabetic ordering. Children are encouraged to learn the alphabet as something to help them to learn to read. But this isn't its main function; the conventional sequence of letters lies behind the making and consulting of *lists*. We treat the alphabetic principle as essential common knowledge and expect everyone to become proficient in its use as early as possible.

The beginnings of looking up, like other aspects of early reading, lie in the playful use of common print. Magazines and catalogues are good examples. For young children the pleasure of turning the pages and distinguishing things familiar and unfamiliar is a particular kind of quest game, hence the popularity of *The Baby's Catalogue*, Janet and Allan Ahlberg's picture-book version of the one from Mothercare. (The discerning adult reader notices the subtlety of the cultural subtext in the different kinds of prams, breakfasts, teas, bedtimes, mums and dads.)

Dictionaries represent a common understanding of what is meant by looking up, as well as a more specific engagement with the activity of finding out. They are usually associated with checking spellings, despite the obvious difficulty in looking for a word you can't spell. Yet dictionaries are by no means in universal use, hence recent computer-led drives to sell them more widely and cheaply. Scrabble players and crossword addicts wear them out, but infrequent users sometimes find that frustration overcomes desire if the information they want is neither evident nor available in the form that would help them.

Teachers know the benefit of getting information quickly, so they teach their pupils a set of procedures for the consultation of reference sources, with special attention to the arrangement of headwords. But if these looking-up exercises are only classroom rituals, the learners are quickly bored, especially if the source book offers little information in return for patient searching. Telling a child to 'look it up' in response to a particularly pressing question is not a good suggestion, unless it comes with an offer of help. Some pupils have never seen a dictionary that shows them how the meanings of words change over time. Others are unaware of the abbreviation conventions, especially the grammatical ones.

The best instances of directed looking happen when the dictionary is used as a means of arbitration in the kinds of arguments the young think are important. Then the usefulness of a dictionary can be demonstrated and the text minutely scrutinized for the required evidence.

Consider, for a moment, just what looking up involves in a context of reading and learning. First, the reader experiences a sense of confusion, a momentary failure of comprehension or some unfamiliarity with a word that the context doesn't make plain. To resolve the difficulty the reader extracts herself or himself from reading that particular text, yet, while reaching for the dictionary or reference book, keeps in mind the meaning of what has already been gleaned so far. Then, having found the appropriate page in a second book, quickly or slowly, the reader engages with a different kind of text and searches for the 'fit' of new information with the unresolved meaning problem still held in the mind. The reader returns to the first text with, or without, the required solution or the desired explanation, and then either proceeds with enlightenment, simply presses on, or, in the case of inexperienced readers, gives up.

Jerome McGann calls this particular looking-up activity 'radial reading', to emphasize that making texts mean is not always a single, linear activity. Instead it is a set of fairly complex reading operations with more than one context.

Ideally, children in school should have a dictionary of their own and access to a range of others, including an up-to-date one. With this in mind, I compared some Oxford University Press dictionaries to see how the selection of meanings might differ in dictionaries designed for use across a school age-range, and thus discern how the dictionary-makers judged 'language development'. Instead, I found that, far from being a 'neutral' source of word definition, the dictionaries betray the same prejudices as many another book of reference. I chose 'female' as my headword and included 'feminine' and 'feminist' in my search. Here are examples from the two most recent editions I found in use. They should be checked against more recent examples in the new edition of the *Concise Oxford Dictionary* (1995).

Oxford Children's Dictionary 1976 (third edition 1993): 'for children of eight upwards':

> **female** *adjective* Of the sex which can give birth to babies or lay eggs.
> **female** *noun* A female person or animal.
> **feminine** *adjective* Belonging to women, suitable for women.
> **feminist** *noun* Someone who believes that women have the same rights as men.

Oxford Senior Dictionary 1982 (second impression 1984): described as 'for students in the upper forms of secondary schools'. The words are taken from textbooks 'to ensure thorough coverage of words encountered as part of the curriculum'. There are notes on spellings, usage and 'proprietary terms'.

> **female** *adj.* 1. of the sex that can bear offspring or produce eggs. 2. (of plants) fruit-bearing, having a pistil and no stamens. 3. of a woman or women.—*n.* a female animal or plant.
> **feminine** *adj.* 1. of or like or suitable for women, having the qualities or appearance considered characteristic of a woman. 2. having the grammatical form suitable for the names of females or for words corresponding to these, *'lioness' is the feminine noun corresponding to 'lion'*—*n.* a feminine word or gender.—**femininity** *n.*
> **feminist**—*n.* a supporter of women's claims to be given rights equal to those of men. **feminism** *n.*

Whose view of feminism is reflected in these entries? When women's magazines use 'feminine', are they referring to something that 'has the appearance considered characteristic of a woman' and nothing more? Like other collections of information, dictionaries reflect the cast of mind of their compilers. Critics who assess dictionaries in their entirety judge, on behalf of lesser literates, the implicit assumptions of the editors.

Children should gradually come to know that all sources of information, including dictionaries, have to be read critically. In this, all adults should be their teachers. Encyclopaedias are not to be regarded as authoritative, either. Selection is the problem for the compilers; for teachers it's the decision whether the purchase of an encyclopaedia gives more children access to more information than a number of other books. This dilemma has become more acute with school purchasing of CD-ROM encyclopaedias. Children use the technology with enthusiasm, but soon discover that, if only one disk is available as the main source for the topic work of a whole class, its limitations become obvious.

Libraries are the places where children discover how books and learning are organized, brought together, so it is important for all who want to help children to learn from books to play some part in teaching them what libraries are good for. For a long time I had no idea that many people feel they cannot use a library because they do not know how to, and are diffident about asking. Certainly you can't love library books as you can those you own. But to consult books in a library is to join the learners, those who know how knowledge is gathered and what the gathering produces. Children need to know that books for learning are, in principle, available to all, but their provision, housing, care and conditions of use have to be safeguarded by those who undertake these things as responsibilities.

Librarians are generally expert in the electronic search systems that young people are eager to use. The computer has become the quickest way of all to inaugurate, carry out and complete certain forms of information search, with the result that pupils are now more inclined to use a screen search than one from a card catalogue. Screen speed is now the normal rate of looking up. Distaste for daunting volumes gives way to competent handling of keyboard devices. But the fundamental question stays the same: what do you do with the information when you get it? What difference

FIVE

School Book Learning

There are three kinds of books in school use: textbooks, course books and topic books. All play a part in children's learning.

In some old textbooks we discover the attraction of book learning when we catch the tone of a writer who wants to communicate enthusiasm as well as knowledge. Hilary Minns discovered Sequel No. II to *The Second Book of Lessons*, which introduced readers to the study of zoology twelve years or so before the publication of *The Origin of Species* in 1859. Here is the second paragraph:

> We will begin with birds. The knowledge of birds is called *Ornithology*, from two words meaning birds and knowledge. This knowledge requires observation, that is, looking about you, and taking notice, rather than learning.
>
> The appearance and habits of birds are most easily studied by those who live in the country. Yet there are several kinds of birds which have no objection to town life, and which may be tamed so as to be quite familiar with the family they belong to.
>
> I knew a duck which lived in the house, and was so attached to the children of the family, that it would follow them about, and walk up stairs into the room where they slept. . . .
>
> There are many things in which birds differ both from men and beasts—some of which you may observe for yourselves, such as—
>
> 1st—In having beaks instead of teeth . . .

As textbooks acquired a unique status in representing the formal discipline of a subject of formal education, they were designed to be memorized in précis form rather than read. Even now, students are expected to learn a subject in the way the book organizes it. Thus, geography texts display how geographers write; business studies conduct business with readers. Across the century or so of compulsory education, textbooks have marched pupils from 'introductory' through 'intermediate' to 'advanced' stages of curriculum subjects which the existence of textbooks helps to define. In many schools textbooks as *compendia* (weighty in content and format, says the dictionary) *are* the curriculum. They demonstrate the authorized, authoritative discourse, the conventional register to be reproduced by the pupils in written work and examinations.

However disguised, the genealogy of most textbooks is that of Dickens's schoolmaster, Gradgrind. The convention is that they contain autonomous statements about some part or aspect of how the world 'really is', and that the writer's knowledge is enough to be learned by pupils in schools. The model textbook is one from which pupils are expected to learn the unchanging nature of French verbs. Wherever there is a formal curriculum for schools with texts recommended by an authority with the power to impose these on teachers, the books are not judged on their merit but in terms of this authority. In book learning this is serious power; it sets textbooks above criticism, even in the educational press.

Teachers feel safe with textbooks and tend to ally themselves with the writers of their choice, even now, when lessons are supported by videos and 'resource packs' of photographs and photocopies. Textbooks are also sources of material for worksheets, exercises that require pupils to 'look up' answers, and, by implication if not in fact, to learn them by memorizing.

Textbooks die hard. Their ossifying factors are the apparently unchanging, institutionalized forms of book learning: grammars in languages; exercises in maths; dates in history; set texts with notes in English literature. To suggest that the inadequacies of textbooks would warrant their removal would be to deny many teachers the props and support of the writers they believe are able to relate subject matter to specific levels of pupil development, year after year. Their benefit is seen as controlling ignorance.

Could schools function without textbooks? I doubt that they would try to. Florence Davies, whose researches emerged in 1986 as *Books in the School Curriculum*, reported that the 'good textbook', described as something which 'facilitates learning', is 'perceived widely as extremely valuable and central to school work by most teachers'. A good textbook has 'appropriate content; it compensates for personal difficulties arising from vocabulary and syntax'. She goes on to suggest that teachers would rather have a textbook than dictate notes. They also believe that different types of text reflect 'different ways of categorizing knowledge' so that the most useful spin-off for a pupil from reading a book is learning *to write in the discourse style and rhetoric of the subject matter* (my italics). Dr Davies also believes that it is possible to detail 'topic types' which give rise to 'distinct information structures and frames' and thus to different kinds of reading.

Other writers, especially those who, like David Olson, recognize the social nature of literacy, are more aware of the restrictive nature of textbooks. As readers are not supposed to argue with them, they are useless for the kind of study which depends on analysis and synthesis, and on thinking about thinking. They also keep other books out of classrooms. As their statements are authorized, writers of textbooks are rarely held responsible for textual misdemeanours, biased judgements or the distortions which come with privileged perspectives. Many issues are passed over in reductive summaries which imply: 'this is what you have to learn, and this is the way you are to learn it.' Textbooks are, in fact, closed books.

Very little has been written about how, or if, textbooks could be different. So it falls to subject advisers to encourage teachers to look at the view of the world that books offer learners. In every textbook I have read there is a hidden curriculum as well as an implicit theory of how children learn. Critical reading soon detects the writers' underlying assumptions about the nature of science, about the humanity or exclusiveness of mathematics, of what counts as evidence in any context. Only where subject teachers read prescribed textbooks in an interrogative fashion is there any chance that they will encourage their students to do the same.

In secondary schools the dominance of the single textbook for subject learning has diminished since the newer forms of examinations have taken into account different styles of learning and teaching. New forms of thematic work have brought different kinds of texts into classrooms, including those of film and video where different ways of reading are acknowledged and different learning styles promoted. The influence of media other than print is constantly at work in modifying older learning practice dependent on printed texts. Interrogative reading of the kind promoted in media studies encourages readers to question their sources. But where teachers read the curriculum documents as *orders*, the authority of textbooks is likely to prevail. Very few textbooks acknowledge that what are offered as *facts* may be differently interpreted. Many schoolbooks conceal the sources of their information: the author is *the* authority.

The textbooks I know best are those designed to offer teachers a complete programme for children learning to read. Since Chall's 1967 research report on teaching methods, the great debate about which pedagogy should prevail has rumbled on, with occasional eruptions. A reading *scheme* offers a package of texts and exercises which teachers administer and pupils perform in a numbered order. Many information-book series follow this model of instruction because the numbering implies sequential learning development. These materials seem to many people to be the triumphs of modern publishing. To others who want children to know what reading is good for, they are a kind of organized impoverishment. The teacher's handbook for reading schemes contains plenty of information about 'reading skills', but little about what makes readers. The worst scenario in reading to learn occurs when children accomplish the tasks set by the textbooks and are then given worksheets of exercises about the 'facts' of things in the world.

Cheaper than textbooks, more modern in design and appearance, course books come in linear series which imply that there is a predictable developmental sequence in pupils' learning: e.g. English I, II, III. Because teachers have rarely been encouraged to resist, or even to examine what the 'experts' are up to, they are disinclined to notice, in a series of repetitious exercises, the fallacy of 'development'.

Course books introduce a topic to be worked through: maths examples, comprehension exercises in English, filling in blanks for learning practice. The rationale is that much learning is repetitious, and pupils are bound to repeat in order to learn and remember. Thus, the argument runs, while most of the class perform these tasks as routines, teachers can devote time to those who have conceptual learning difficulties.

The great weakness of course books designed as lessons is that they are essentially *normative*. Every pupil answers the same questions, gets the same right answers. There is never a full exploration of topic material, very little continuous text for extended reading, not enough material to engage readers in the dialogues of topic discourse and even too little opportunity to practise it. What there is, is a series of tasks which the learners *perform* and then move on to the next lot, glad to have finished but unreflective about what has been learned, if anything at all. Again, it is the world in bits, in closed books.

Textbooks are written to be authoritative, to stand alone. They declare what counts as a subject to be learned and are also related to the exclusive power of external examinations. Course books are school 'course work', designed to familiarize pupils with the words of authority in the subject. Topic books are hybrid. They can be about any part of any subject, treated in different ways, using all the resources of printing.

The authority of topic books lies in creating and maintaining interest in matters which are as likely to be selected by the readers as by their teachers. Writers are encouraged to use language informally, showing rather than telling, by using the illustrations as part of their text. Since they emerged as the result of primary school teachers' dissatisfaction with their teaching books in the 1950s, their number has increased greatly, throughout all levels of schooling, not least because the publishers discovered the profits in packaging books as series. Over the years producers of topic books have tried to link both the pupil's and the teacher's personal knowledge to the more authoritative material in books: the visit to the lions in the zoo and lions in the wider world on the page; the ingredients of home cooking and their growth in far-flung fields; the relics of history and their origins in the past.

Topic books constitute a well recognized genre. An American scholar, Christine Pappas, read one hundred children's information books so as to distinguish the 'obligatory elements' of the kind that linguists say establish a genre as a recognizable kind of writing. The first of these elements is the *topic presentation*. It announces the subject in general. The second is the *representation of attributes*. These describe the parts of the topic subject. The third element is *characteristic events*, where the topic can be seen in operation. I tried this out on a book called *What is a Bird?* It fitted the model exactly.

There are also two 'optional elements' in Pappas' analysis of the typical information book: *category comparison*, when there are illustrations of different kinds of the same thing, e.g. different birds' eggs and beak shapes, and a *final summary*, just as you'd expect. I find this a useful way of looking at a topic book for two reasons. First, because so many books follow this pattern, it shows how entrenched is the notion of the *structure of learning* in the production of information books. The richly resourced and researched volumes from Dorling Kindersley, and all the innovative presentation work this publishing house has done with great success to interest both children and adults in learning about the world in books, are structured on this model. Second, if any book does not conform to this reading structure, there must be a different idea of book learning behind it.

What is a Bird? is a good example of the art of design in modern topic books. Each photograph has an explanatory caption of up to three sentences and some of the information in the captions is also in the principal text, which occupies a quarter of the space of each doublespread. The caption texts are likely to be read first as they sit next to the pictures. They provide the names of the individual birds or explain a special close-up feature, such as the hooks that hold contour feathers and the waterproofing of goose feathers. There is no doubt about the attraction such facticity holds for young inquiring readers.

The principal text is more problematic. The reader has to 'chord' its statements with the pictured examples in a different way from the words of the captions, in order to build up the relation of the parts of the text into an understanding of the whole topic as represented by the book.

My experience of reading many beautifully illustrated topic books is that the writing is a kind of adjunct, showing different ways of labelling what is to be looked at. Having cancelled at the outset the reader's implicit understanding of birds gained from experience of city sparrows, ducks on ponds, seagulls, house martins in the eaves, and offered instead the exotic plumage of the albatross as an exciting example of feathers, does the writer of *What is a Bird?* leave the reader to make the inference that the birds he or she knows are just as intriguing as the parrot, the penguin, the flamingo and the ostrich in the book? It is difficult to tell.

Even very competent readers need help if they have no experience of a subject and meet it first in its book form. In contrast, quite young readers, who are well informed about a topic that interests them, can move into high-gear reading of a complex text. This is what teachers see and know. The problem is that teachers are rarely given the chance to turn their knowledge of how their pupils learn from books into the kinds of *understandings*, as well as descriptions of pedagogy, that other teachers can profit from. When teachers are given a chance to explain their interactions with readers and topic texts in lessons, they offer distinctive kinds of evidence about book learning.

In *Language Matters*, the journal of the Centre for Language in Primary Education, Julie Asquith reports her experience of introducing children to the use of topic books as models for their own research and writing. She shows how a pupil 'happily read away, using a range of books, becoming more familiar with the more orthodox names for plant parts . . . and kept reading pieces of information to her friends and to myself. She added a number of both appropriate and inappropriate pieces of text to her work.' At her teacher's suggestion, this young learner wrote a second account 'which synthesized the first-hand experience and the book research'. (Note the tolerance, at the first stage of a nine-year-old's writing, of 'inappropriate pieces of text'.)

In the same issue of the journal, another teacher, Sue Adler, asks the complex, necessary question: 'Whose reality does a history, social science or geography book portray?' She goes on to explore 'the subjectivity and potentially controversial viewpoint' of all topic books:

> . . . whether this is the shape of the world's continents, information on Islam, causes of wars, droughts and disease, clothes and costumes, castles or food. The background, beliefs and attitudes of authors, illustrators and publishers, are all factors affecting the information given to children. How children receive and interpret the information is just as diverse, for similar reasons.

Teachers also know children discover early that the characteristic topic book *names* things. Like poets, children cherish this as an endeavour. Also, their curiosity is insatiable, so it is never true to say that they are empty-headed. When they feel they know something, they care about its worth and authenticity. When they can read fluently, their mental energy lets them soak up undifferentiated information before it is sorted out into generic categories, hence the success of *The Guinness Book of Records*. There is no evidence that children learn from books in predictable, calculable ways, so we need more informal details about how children learn from topic books. Conversations with them reveal that they make 'habitable' categories in their thinking about subjects that interest them. As far as our knowledge goes, it seems safe to say that, quite early in their schooldays, some boys and girls begin to prefer books of information to stories. This is treated as normal in boys and exceptional in girls.

We still need much more evidence of the kind of mental 'space' that readers inhabit as they read to learn, the different reasons they have for accepting or rejecting what books tell them, and the ways with words that turn understanding into knowing. If, however, we agree that significant texts teach readers not only that they *can* learn but also how to enter into an interior dialogue with a more informed knower, then something may come from a closer inspection of the kinds of invitation offered by writers (or, as is now more usual, makers) of individual texts across a range of subject matters.

SIX

Reading and Learning by Design

The most noteworthy schoolbook of the Enlightenment was *Orbis Pictus*, the world in pictures, by John Amos Comenius, published in English in 1659. It was the culmination of the life's work of this gentle Moravian, who was persuaded that if children learned about the world in greater detail, they would grow up in temperate tolerance of others. So he gave his readers woodcut pictures as representations of the world of their time because, he says, 'there was nothing in the understanding which was not before in the sense'. His main concern was to help children enjoy learning 'till the thing be sufficiently discerned'.

The idea of *representation* not only persists but is central to whatever counts as book learning. In pictures, designs and diagrams, and whatever else is 'graphic'—that is, written—learners see things from the world as two-dimensional forms and learn from them as if they were present and actual. Think, then, of how much modern picture books for school learning have in common with glossy magazines, catalogues and coloured newspaper supplements with their publicity semiotics. Nowadays designers of books for learning pay as much attention, sometimes more, to what readers look at as to what they read. Learning from words and pictures in the early years of primary school seems both intellectually and culturally straightforward, especially if the reader's early experience has included a range of picture books by skilful artists and writers. In fact, this learning is selectively manipulated.

One result of current emphases on the design of books of information is that they are rarely the composition of a single author or artist. Instead they involve the kind of teamwork usually associated with the making of films and television programmes and the mounting of exhibitions. The enhanced use of computer techniques is well to the fore in all of these, which reminds us that, although the content of books of information may be running ahead of the learners, young readers are often more aware of how the print and pictures come together than their teachers are. There is no doubt that the design features of television programmes and advertisements influence topic-book producers in their efforts to attract readers. It is important to note, however, that children's picture story books have a different, longer history.

The publishing house of Dorling Kindersley has set new standards of topic-book production against which buyers of books for schools now measure most others. Their promotional booklet, *Eyewitness, a Universal Language for Learning*, is interesting because it offers a theory of learning from books composed mainly of photographs.

The intention of *Eyewitness* is to present excellent photographs arranged for learning in terms of all possible topics: birds, trees, whales, time, space and all the 'periods' of history. Think of a topic and there will be a book to match it. Teams of experts who have access to the latest technologies 'explode' photographs by spreading or anatomizing them. Specialists are consulted about the topic details. Educators judge the 'level' of the presentation. Source managers seek out information and representative artefacts in their most authentic and authoritative forms. Graphic designers, art and series editors add to the list of credits. The book format is the traditional double-page spread. The result is a series of volumes with brilliant white pages—Dorling Kindersley are emphatic about this as a *quality* of the production. The distinctive feature of each page is the absence of shadows.

Dorling Kindersley have also coined the term 'lexigraphics' to denote the interaction of reproduced photographs, drawings, diagrams and print. They call it a 'universal language' that speaks to the readers at many levels. Here is how the originators of lexigraphics promote book learning.

> We think it's like fluoride in toothpaste—you can't see it but you don't want toothpaste without it. In the same way, the special ingredients in a lexigraphic book need to be pointed out before you appreciate their benefits.

I don't doubt the educational integrity of the publishers, but until now it has been unusual to market learning in this way. The implicit message to other educators is: you have to look at children learning in the world rather than from books if you are to help them to use books to learn. These books go beyond linear print. The claim is that, by showing the world 'as it is', photographs become a 'natural' language.

To examine claims for the effectiveness of lexigraphics you need the Eyewitness pamphlet that accompanies the series. In it, the rationale is that the pictures are presented in great detail to 'slow down the looking', in ways not possible on television, so that the reader investigates the details on the page, and, at the same time, to 'speed up the reading' by keeping the words close to the icons and making the bursts of printed text as short as possible, so as to fix what the reader sees in his or her memory.

I am now looking at the 'dominant icon', a full-page, detailed photograph of an owl's wing, in *Eyewitness Guide: Birds*. I have never before seen a picture of a bird's wing in such close-up, and I am unlikely to see it in actuality. On the next page, the 'primary' level of information 'analyses the component parts of the icon', that is, the articulation of the wing is compared with the movement of the human arm. 'Supplementary' information comes as a series of related topics and photographs of different sizes: birds in flight and Leonardo da Vinci's drawing for a flight machine. Readers are to 'integrate what they see with what they already know'. The function of the words is to 'authenticate the picture', that is, to prove its credibility: to persuade the readers that what they are carefully looking at is 'the case'.

In the tradition of illustrated books for children this is a turnaround. The conventional expectation has hitherto been that the pictures would support the authority of the words. As a result of familiarity with Dorling Kindersley books, children expect this degree of verisimilitude. But the detailed components of the book design and of the contents have a *literalness*, a notion that things exist as they are, without even the witness of the human eye behind the camera. This seems to infer that learning about them can be equally direct and that it is right to exclude the imaginative interpretations most children bring to their book learning.

Compare, if you will, the Eyewitness endeavour with a book about paintings by Robert Cumming called *Just Look* . . . After the Introduction, where he tells his readers that he is 'going to show you some of the many different ways artists make pictures and how they help us share their ways of looking', he asks his readers:

How many paintings do you think there are in this book? Before you start to count, look very carefully at this famous picture. It was painted by an Italian, Paolo Veronese, over 400 years ago, and it shows Jesus's first miracle, turning water into wine at Cana. If you can find a magnifying glass, you will be able to examine it very closely indeed. (8)

On the next page the gentle trick is revealed: 'You see, there are no actual paintings in this book, only printed reproductions.' *Just Look* . . . helps its readers to become aware of what they are looking at and to consider what they think they see. They then begin to understand the nature of representations and how representations make meanings.

My concern is not to discredit photography nor to belittle the achievements of those who have used it to make children's topic books into windows on the world. But my appreciation of lexigraphics stops short of my acceptance of it as 'a universal language'. It is as culture-bound as any other semiotic system, and reminds me of a Frank Smith aphorism: 'reality is the fantasy we live by'.

At the same time, there are certain things that photographs can never represent. *Incredible Cross-Sections* is the product of Stephen Biesty's skilled draughtsmanship in representations of eighteen buildings in cutaway drawings. The illusion is that the outer layers of each object have been peeled back to reveal the complicated innards of masterworks of technology and design created by human beings for the furtherance of travel, art, work and war.

Before they open the book, readers are invited to 'see, learn and discover'. You 'see the insides of one of the world's largest telescopes'; learn 'what a tank looks like inside'; discover 'what holds up the Empire State building'. The details link searching (where is the loo?) with sequencing (where does the drill head meet the oil?), recognition (so that's what a solar is), and surprise (all that for just one opera). Readers discover what they may not even have considered in the everyday: how air gets into a subway, that astronomers look into mirrors to see the sky, why skyscrapers don't fall down in high winds, how cramped, dark and smelly is life in a submarine or down a mine. With Biesty readers work out why spiral staircases rise clockwise and that the boredom on a galleon was probably the same as on an oilrig.

This is learning as adventure, almost entirely male.

When I think of all the trouble we take to help children to understand the writing system I wonder at our apparently casual view of reading diagrams. They crop up in almost every information book I've looked at for children over eight. Just exactly how to turn two-dimensional drawings into understandings of three-dimensional objects is not explained in anything I have read. The contrary operation, drawing a diagram of a process or an object, is assumed to be possible for children before they are in their teens. I haven't seen a book that teaches them how to do it, but presumably some learn in what are now 'technology' lessons or in modern pedagogies for mathematics.

References to children reading diagrams include words such as 'puzzling over' them. This doesn't mean that diagrams give children problems; they enjoy them as puzzles to be worked out. Computer games are composed of diagrammatic operations. But Margaret Mallett is right when she says that most children need help in interpreting them in books where the accompanying description assumes that the reader has the same viewpoint as the maker of the diagram.

Diagrammatic representations of a piece of machinery, such as a canal lock, or of scientific processes like the circulation of the blood, the nitrogen cycle or the double helix of DNA, all appear in school topic books on the assumption that the readers will have learned about them in lessons and now will stop to sort out how they 'work' by following the diagram arrows or by reconstructing the indications of the relationships of the parts to the whole. But we have very little evidence of what diagram readers really do.

Unlike words in sentences, diagrams cannot be read aloud. Only when learners are encouraged to explain how they interpret the drawings does the teacher discover what they have understood. My guess is that many parents have interpreted to their children the intricacies of a canal lock when all that the text offers is 'Barges use locks to move to higher or lower parts of the canal.' In most photographs the canal seems flat. 'Use' is doubtful; the locks are part of the canal, not of the barges. Often the arrow symbols are ambiguous; what they point to, or away from, is not always clear.

Professional diagram-makers—engineers, architects, surveyors and the like—learn the diagrammatic tricks of their trade in the contexts of their use. Those for whom diagrams are 'models' know at once whether the system will work because, for them, the operation displayed by a drawing is a representation of experienced understanding.

For children, it is difficult to look at a series of lines and then read a sentence which says that the light of a laser beam is 'narrowed'. My vision of this includes my microwave oven, but I had to learn from the dictionary that a laser is a 'device for converting light of mixed frequencies into an intense, narrow, monochromatic beam of coherent light'.

Until I know better and discover more, I'm left with the impression that most young readers who make immediate sense of diagrams are confirming rather than discovering things. In mathematics and science lessons they are given practice in making diagrammatic interpretations of what is less clearly represented in language. Visitors to the Science Museum explain diagrams to each other and enjoy those the Museum provides as a kind of advanced adult game. More people than ever now discuss DIY instructions. The increased emphasis on technology in schoolwork and the use of computers for diagram-making will change the situation beyond my comprehension. This is as far as I can go, except to say that books for learning need to inform their readers about the diagrammatic systems they expect them to understand as a means to interpret their content, not least in the matters of scale.

When complex communications, transport and travelling enter our lives, map-reading becomes a necessary part of book learning and is a genuine modern literacy. Long before they are expected to know anything of the abstractions of map-making, children draw lines, plans and maps as a significant kind of play. From adventure stories, especially in the graphic mode, like *Tintin*, they learn about maps leading to buried treasure. We know this because they sometimes talk as they trace the outline. Then they explain what 'this is', or 'where it goes' to an interested adult. A simple drawing of a house may have a garden path up to the front door. It is called a 'road' because 'people go there'. Myra Barrs, who has studied children's 'maps of play', says that the map-makers orient themselves in both the world they know and in the one for which they make images. As they draw, children impose both meaning and feeling on the image at the point of the moving pencil. They see maps as a place to be. By drawing as they talk, they are also learning to write in the sense of 'compose' rather than 'copy'. That is, they are making imaginary worlds.

Children's early map drawings may seem far removed from the operations of the Ordnance Survey, but all kinds of map-making are part of our habits of making visual representations of the world so as to set it in order. The most sophisticated conventionalized maps imply those of early childhood. In their pre-school drawings children are free to choose the map form and its contents without reference to the world outside their heads. When they encounter maps in books they have to orient themselves to the writer's description of the topography in order to understand what the map is there to show and tell. The map-maker assumes that any reader will enter the map at any point. Each individual map-user orients herself or himself to the significant district or distance. How does this work? I haven't discovered, for the simple reason that no one offered me any explanation.

So now for my revised map-reading in terms of how children learn to do it. In primary school they are encouraged to make simple sketches of familiar routes and to locate known landmarks. Teachers then discover how many of the mapping conventions the children are familiar with. This exercise is always popular, done with alacrity. Some discussion uncovers that under the surface of the pupils' consciousness there are alternative worlds of the imagination, detailed, clear, peopled. I wonder then if, when they and I look at 'real' maps, we see the world as marked by lines, but empty?

Many books of information, not only those on geographical topics, include maps; very few instruct the reader how to look at them. One can tell what proves difficult to explain by the number of books on the same topic: the rotation of the earth, the movements of tides, the location of towns in relation to communication and supply routes. The multitudes of named diagrams assume that children will follow what they represent. I can't believe that this is how children learn about day and night, the phases of the moon and the differences in climate. The makers of these maps and drawings must assume that the reader has already had some kind of understanding of the processes, and the map is a kind of image to hold together the naming of parts.

One writer tackled the problem directly. Using studies in cognitive psychology, David Scott made a three-stage theory of visualization to distinguish *map reading*, extracting meaning from maps, on the model of looking up word meanings in a dictionary; *map analysis*, using the information; *map interpretation*, using our experience of the world. He suggests that we do all of these things at once, presumably if we are experienced. But static explanations don't help us to discover how children come to know how to do these things. Other writers concentrate on defining or describing the words of the map-makers' code: location, direction, scale, distance, or they interpret legends to discern places, routes, populations, the relation of people to the environment. No writers of map books I read problematized the difficulties experienced by young readers or frustrated adults. Having seen what happens when a blank map is handed out in a classroom, I know that the right way up isn't always evident if there are no words on the page. Some children fail to separate the sea from the land because the conventions are never made clear.

How should we describe the visuals of maps so that learners can come to an interpretive understanding of what maps mean? For example, on maps of ocean currents there are lines that look like waves coming in towards the land. That is not how they are to be 'scientifically' read. Can an intelligent reader make sense of this without some understanding of the movement of the seas? School libraries don't provide for potential navigators, unless this is a regional specialism. Then I realized that many children nowadays have been in an aeroplane. They have had a bird's-eye view of the surface of the globe. Does this make a difference to their understanding of how it becomes a drawing? At the end of my book search for lessons in map-reading I had still more questions than answers.

Our technologies for making maps seem to have outstripped our ability to help children to read them. Probably the best lessons come from the daily weather forecasts on television, with winds whirling round, the same signs always for rain and clouds, and words to explain what is being demonstrated. Viewers in Norfolk and Northern Ireland have different ways of looking, dictated by their situated perspectives. That's probably as good a starting point as any.

As in all other aspects of book learning, adults who want children to be at ease with modern, complicated *graphigraphies* (a twentieth-century word coined on the model of *literacies*) have to spend more time discussing with them how pictures of the world are made in different kinds of mapping codes, and encouraging them to enlarge their horizons. At present I am not convinced that there are topic books which help them very much to do this before secondary school, and, even then, the onus must be on their teachers to find better books to link their experiences to their learning.

As a topic on its own, reading and learning by design covers a wide field of study of how the eyes and the brain work together to let us perceive things, and how conceptual understandings develop from habits of perception. Here I have done little more than declare how much is taken for granted about the ways children are expected to learn from graphics, photographs, diagrams and maps and the place of representations of various kinds in their coming to know as they read. As visual literacies become more talked about, and the role of semiotics in public life becomes better understood, we shall have to discover more about the part these things play in book learning.

SEVEN

Time Lines: History book learning

History is the great narrative, the story we tell ourselves and each other about the past that lets us anticipate the future, while we live in a time we imagine and call the present.

For much of childhood reading, history is a series of storied events. The difference between history and other narratives is that history lives with its partner, memory, especially folk memory. Most knowledge includes this memory, as learning includes remembering. My first teachers said we had to ask when, where, who, why and what about past events recorded in books. Under instruction we diligently asked these questions, but the only acceptable answers were those the book supplied or the teacher's dictation summarized. Book chapters were time sections. They began with causes: of the Reformation, the Civil War, and ended with results: the rise of Presbyterianism, the execution of Charles I. The *who* were mostly monarchs, generals or politicians; the *where* was usually England after 1603; the *when* was a list of dates for events all over the world; *what* and *why* linked the causes with the effects in ways never questioned. It seemed unlikely that everyday events, like going to school, were ever linked to these great happenings.

When, and how, do you think, children discover that they are part of history, that the time lines of their lives coincide with those of events officially recorded in the modern equivalents of annals and chronicles? This understanding is simply assumed by writers of history topic books for use in school. Perhaps the early understanding of how 'once upon a time' is linked in a particular way with 'ever after' in most stories extends this narrative pattern to 'centuries'. In my case Scottish history was all around me: the burial place of kings, sites where martyrs were burned, borders disputed. I learned most of these events in songs and ballads where no questions are asked. There was no way I could separate in my memory the novels of Scott and Stevenson from the book account of Jenny Geddes's protest at the introduction of Laud's prayer book in the Scots kirk. They were all equally 'true'.

The other question is: when do young learners discover that there is more than one way to interpret the past? My teachers, 1930s radicals, were sure that the execution of Charles I ended the tyranny of 'The Divine Right of Kings', although my book spoke of his 'martyrdom'. My vision of the French Revolution in history lessons was of a popular triumph, a view not shared by the author of *A Tale of Two Cities*. What alerts the young to the silences of historians? No one ever told me about the Clearances of the Highlands, although some of my classmates were surely the kith and kin of the dispossessed. Brecht's question, 'Where did all the masons go / When the Great Wall of China was finished?' was not on my list of 'wheres'.

I belabour these instances for two reasons. First, a school curriculum—especially a national one—in history will be as positioned in its viewpoint as any single history book. Then, my recollected experience and that of others suggest that history comes to us clad in the manner of its telling. For me, history is directly related to what we still call literature. I was well out of my teens before I realized that history is aback of all things, but there is no single, straightforward version of it that has complete authority for all learners. When I came to live in London I soon discovered that the notion of being British rarely included the Scots. My condition of exile and encounters with others whose language was not English prompted extended reading against the taken-for-granteds in conventional school history. 'Reading England', as a place with a past, is as much the business of critical reading as *Areopagitica*.

'In order to qualify as "historical", an event must be susceptible to at least two narrations of its occurrence' (19). The words are Hayden White's; he suggests that, 'By becoming a narrative history gains formal coherence, but not the total "reality", that which depends upon our imaginations'. Each narration is given a formal ending (the death of kings, the treaties at the end of wars) that includes a moral (the war to end all wars; the need for global understanding). Then White says, 'It is the historians themselves who have transformed narrativity from a *manner of speaking* [my italics] into a paradigm of the form which reality itself displays to a "realistic" consciousness' (23). We are expected to believe that we can really understand the past by being told about it.

54

Spoken history is the version of the local past children acquire from their elders, including their teachers. Written history is another retelling. It can extend the framework of a report to include either a longer time line or a wider scene of contemporary reference, or both. Historians have longed to make history objective, like science, a serious discipline which depends on the logical analysis of material evidence: chronicles, records, diaries, accounts, laws; in short, written records instead of memory. In presenting history to the young, these makers of topic books tend to assume that the past displays itself when enough events, artefacts and documents are collected and related. So lessons are given as singular accounts of what happened, when there are clearly many versions. Even the most careful eyewitnesses disagree. The death of President Kennedy was seen by many people; the reports seem to suggest that he was shot from a particular place. Even after seeing film footage many times I wonder how anyone can be sure about what happened.

If you want to see how historians incorporate a point of view in their account of the past, read Barbara Tuchman's study of the fourteenth century, called *A Distant Mirror*. It was written in 1978. Her amazing ordering and analysis of the complicated events of that period of the Black Death, 'the most lethal disaster in recorded history', were undertaken to show that the human species had been through 'worse' than the threat of nuclear holocaust which preoccupied the United States during the period of the Cold War when the book was being written.

Without a historian's authority, but with a reader's interest in writing, I offer some glimpses of texts about 'the past' as ways of seeing and telling. Other readings include autobiography and biography and historical novels. History books form the largest single topic-book section in school libraries, and most of those I have read suggest that the authors' difficulties include a massive uncertainty, which takes various forms, about how to 'pitch' the rhetoric of the subject matter so that the reader is persuaded about the 'actuality' of the events. No author directly tells young learners that a single book cannot contain all that is known in great detail about the historical past, especially the social past. Any national curriculum for history teaching that says sources should always be questioned would be a great step forward.

I began my reading by revisiting some old textbooks of my

school years to find where I learned that the Romans built roads and established the sites of towns; how the New World was 'discovered'; that monarchic succession was important; that wars are recurrent, with the implied notion that they demonstrate male bravery and national superiority; that government is about taxes. From an account of the Indian Mutiny I realized how views of 'olden times', implanted early, remain as cultural compost in later judgements. School history nowadays, with its emphasis on considering differences in sources of evidence, seems light years away from the simplistic notion of 'progress' that defined my early learning. Yet the chapters in many of the books produced to support the growth of historical understanding are still shaped as incidents, episodes or examples, that is, as lessons. Someone should undertake an analysis of them in terms of their relation to social and political emphases, and their views on the nature of the human condition which we all share. Do acknowledged historians, I wonder, investigate the school roots of their own perspectives on the past and encourage their students to do the same?

Most of the pre-examination texts in history are designed to make some contact with the interests of pupils who can read independently. But the implied readers of most school history books are teachers, those whose advice was first sought by the commissioning editors; hence the predominance of collections and series. Most texts have a trustworthy specificity. Many of them can be read aloud to a class to demonstrate history as a time line. But few, if any, of those prepared for pre-teen children acknowledge the situated perspective of the writers. A general assumption is that history can be divided into periods, a major stretch of time for 'core texts' (*The Roman World*), and subdivided into 'topics' for special interest inquiries (*The Roman Army*), which children are encouraged to undertake as part of a topic study.

There are also 'supplementary study units' to reinforce the pupils' books and the teachers' resource books. The quality of products such as these depends on the investment made by the publishing house, the skill and knowledge of writers, editors, designers, set against the school's willingness and ability to pay what the books cost. Book learning in history, in this form, comes packaged, annotated, complete and, therefore, safe. Many of these sets are up-to-date in their format and content. But in terms of their authority, they assume rather than expose what counts as historical *learning*. The question is, therefore, whose views prevail as part of what is taught, read and learned?

Outside the structured edifice of a school curriculum, books of historical information seem to have slipped their moorings and bob about on a topical sea. Here, again, is the problem of how reading becomes understanding. Suppose you want to study World War II so as to introduce the learners to different kinds of evidence, to invite them to examine what they have 'picked up' from TV films and the like. You will discover that there is no clear schoolbook distinction between primary and secondary sources. How do the readers interpret a page of a newspaper reproduced as an illustration? What kind of lead does the author give? An authoritative example of writing about World War II is a compendium of recollections of evacuation. *Goodnight Children, Everywhere* uses photographs and letters, drawings and posters through which the voices of the storytellers come loud and clear. This is primary source material recovered in a book. To encounter it is to see recorded experiences as historical evidence. What it feels like to take part in a battle is best understood by reading novels.

The editorial habit of slicing time into centuries cuts readers off from seeing that history is not so divided. English social life was still Victorian after the queen was dead, while the changes in scientific and biblical thinking, for example, which are commonly regarded as recent, had begun long before her diamond jubilee.

In looking at a great number of history books for learners I remembered an article by Robert Hull in which he comments on 'the extractive dental form of reading'. He adds, 'there are far too few history books for young people to read'. Although the publishers' lists may seem to contradict him, I know he is right. In his book *The Language Gap* Hull gives the redlight warning example of what happens in history lessons, an instance oft repeated in texts which try to simplify complex situations. A conscientious young teacher wants her pupils to understand the difficulties that faced Queen Elizabeth I on her accession. As the school textbook is proving impenetrable—the details overwhelm the ideas—the teacher tries to provide a diagrammatic interpretation of the Queen's political dilemmas. Hull discussed with her 'children's problems generally in understanding history', then reports:

The simplifying that she had decided on involved a kind of précis, turning the continuous 'difficult text' into a number of discrete 'main points' that could be 'put over visually'. Thus, the group of problems faced by Elizabeth was translated by means of a metaphoric model into a group of *boulders* on the *road* to the future. She had asked pupils [twelve-year-olds] to fill in the spaces (represented by the boulders) 'with their own ideas' about the topics . . . The textbook phrase 'The country was poor, there was no money in the Treasury' becomes 'shortage of money' in the model. The accessibility of the notion of a whole country being poor remained unexamined. What it means to say a country is 'poor' is, of course, an exploration in itself. Equally compressed notions like 'vast unemployment', 'the threat from France and Spain', and 'the religious problem' have to be handled as well. (71)

About the teacher's diagram Hull says: 'Unless the metaphor is explicated, it may be that pupils have the notion of *im*movable objects in their heads. Their *in*surmountability may be what is learnt: Elizabeth did not solve her problems.'

For some time children learning to handle the complexities of history books and to express them as part of their own understanding have to make statements that only approximate to what historians would take to be the case. The problem for readers begins with the writers' difficulties in relating the 'big shapes' of historical time to the minutiae of any given event. In a reading situation, as in a teaching one, children need more information, not less, an accretion of interesting detail rather than a précis of events, but they also need to grasp the connections and the different kinds of significance implied by the writer. They need storytellers for at least some of the time they are becoming aware of what history is, instead of collecting information in preparation for examinations.

Pupils soon learn that history comes with a particular tune of telling:

Edward reached Reims in the first week of December, presumably expecting the city to admit him after what was to have been his victorious advance. Forewarned of his intention, Reims had been strengthening its walls during the long preparation and remained stubbornly closed, forcing the English into a siege. (Tuchman 187)

No reader stops to ask if a town can actually strengthen its walls, or if 'what was to have been' was a bad guess on the part of the writer. History books are full of sentences such as 'The merchants believed they had been deprived of their rights', and the reader is left to guess who deprived them or if the beliefs were mistaken. We are back again at 'the country was poor'. Schoolbooks sort out these problems by ignoring them, their authors having been told that simple statements are best. Again, what teachers see as readers' problems are often writers' carelessness.

Although they may not notice ambiguities in sentence construction, young historians do begin to be aware of differences in the writers' approaches to a topic. This is usually more characteristic of secondary school pupils, but it is possible to let younger ones see that there is no unified view of what happened during events like the early years of the French Revolution, when 'the people' is a more complicated idea than most books suggest. As the result of much emphasis in school on medieval farming, many British children believe that, generally, 'in the olden days' most people lived on farms. In scores of books about the Industrial Revolution in England, the upheavals, changes and social disturbances are sorted into singular topics: inventions, railways, factories, trade, towns. The details are roughly the same in each.

School history books offer readers comparisons between what they see in the world around them and what it 'was like' at various times in the past in terms of schools, houses or jobs, and 'conditions' are presented as instances of change. The authenticities we recognize in autobiographies and diaries *can* be found in books like Sheila Sancha's *Walter Dragun's Town*, where the fiction of a wealthy Florentine merchant visiting Stanford (now Stamford) to buy raw wool is used to show the economic life of the town at the time of Edward I.

The crowded immediacy of children's awareness of current events suggests that they need a whole skein of tales to arrive at some kind of insight into the felt life of an historical period. We now have many different, detailed versions of the same events, stored electronically or offered as TV programmes. Evidence is so abundant that it needs much more sifting. Disagreement about which details are important is of less concern than false reporting of sources. History may become more long-winded, but not necessarily more 'true'. Paradoxically, we also want our history sooner, hence the brisk trade in the memoirs of politicians, rock stars and others whose lasting qualities are not predictable.

Narrative accounts of the lives of notable people written for young readers are generally disappointing at this time when biography for adults is so clearly flourishing. Social awareness and meticulous research, laced with psychological subtlety and delivered in skilled writing, have re-created biography in English almost as a new literary genre that crosses many fields of interest.

Even if we discount length and detail, very few significant biographies are written for confident young readers or adolescents, who seek the details about their current heroes and heroines in the magazines of fan clubs, linked to more exploitative kinds of information giving. The style of these ephemera is carried over into books, but where photographs take up most of the space there is little scope for the kind of encounter with a life and ideas that a mature biography makes possible.

Other difficulties arise when the writer uses the person written about to represent a bigger topic. Thus, Michelangelo becomes 'the Renaissance', Marie Curie stands for scientific research into atoms and radium to represent women's contribution to twentieth-century progress. Darwin *is* evolution. The human interest in Steve Parker's *Darwin and Evolution* is in the details of Darwin's undistinguished schooldays and his voyage on *The Beagle*, but see how the writer's concern to bring his subject up to date means abandoning the biographical material in favour of a banal, over-generalized, even confusing summary.

> Evolution generally takes a long time. It happens over hundreds of generations, and thousands or millions of years. Many scientists assumed it was a gradual and continuing process.
>
> In the 1970s, a newer idea said that evolution may happen in fits and starts. Species stay the same for a very long time. Then they change rapidly in a burst of evolution, over a relatively short time, before settling down again. The theory is called punctuated equilibrium. It may be important in some groups of animals or plants, and it is still being discussed. (27)

How long is a short time if evolution takes thousands or millions of years? This lack of specificity makes topic books boring. The most difficult thing for young learners to grasp is the time line of evolution and the nature of evolutionary change in relation to changes in themselves as they grow. In school writing, for example, they are well aware of the nature of the 'correct' explanations of Darwinian hypotheses, but their personal constructs of historical time are often still in the early stages. History teachers confront learners' confusions when books have too many gaps in their texts. For example, some of the readers I consulted had obviously got the idea that Darwin 'invented' evolution. The notion of a theory being a kind of informed guess about some recurrent evidence had not been part of the book or lesson material.

My concern is not to take issue with individual volumes but to show that the writing of history information books for pupils to read on their own is a difficult business. New printing techniques produce illustrations of such high quality that original documents, photographs of contemporary artefacts, and pictures of famous men and women seem to make the-past-in-the-present more immediate. But the result may be a shortening of *interpretative text* that would fit the bits of information together, and so make possible more coherent understandings in the readers.

How, for example, do we learn about a civilization? Learning about a civilization is the reason usually given for involving pupils under the age of twelve in bookish details about the ancients: Greeks, Romans, Incas, Aztecs and Egyptians. The material remains of these peoples have encouraged archaeologists, historians, linguists, film-makers and the ordinarily curious to reconstruct their social lives, warfare, literature, fine art, and philosophies, all of which flourished while their contemporaries in other places were living in caves. Now, in museums and from travelling exhibitions, the general public can see some of the relics far from their place of origin, and muse on the flourishing and dissolution of the works of dwellers in great ancient cities. What do we think our children should learn about them?

In order to characterize this kind of book learning I chose Ancient Egypt as the focus of my reflections, wondering the while what children in modern Cairo now learned about the Sphinx. I found less to interest readers starting this topic from scratch than I had hoped. The books are full of colourful and interesting pictures, but no writer seems to want to ask, even implicitly, how young learners could get some kind of alert purchase on the distant past by looking at the objects that have survived. They need to have human life blown into them. Only on a large illustrated time-line poster, part of the material produced with the *Eyewitness Guide to Ancient Egypt*, was there some indication of how to see the passage of time as 'periods'—a historian's trick and not part of the Egyptians' understanding—and how to count over the line that separates BC from AD. How should we explain to those whose memories are short, whose view of the past is still in the making, that the oldest pyramids and the mystery of the Sphinx (c. 3000 BC and later) were as ancient to Cleopatra, the last Egyptian queen, as the ancient Greeks are to us?

History needs the coherence of narrative to bring together characters and events. The Egyptians enter our culture in two sets of tales: one about the pharaohs and the pyramids, the other as the history of the Jews. From the latter we learn about their captivity in Egypt and their escape across the Red Sea. (How do you explain the parting of the waters?) In the former we come to know the burial practices of the kings, which, by all accounts, seem to have taken the lifetime of each one to accomplish. The giant pyramids remain to convey the Ozymandian message: 'Look on my works, ye Mighty, and despair!' Is that the moral of it all?

The best use I have found of original sources is in the book I just mentioned, the *Eyewitness Guide to Ancient Egypt*. Carefully designed pages in full colour make the book a treasure trove for finding out. The time line runs from before the pharaohs to the seventh century AD. Besides being an introduction for beginners, the book is good preparation for looking at the original objects in the British Museum. There the study goes into its second phase: what the archaeologists learned from their discoveries and what the historians now think it is important to know. 'This vase was carved from mottled stone called *breccia* using flint or copper tools. Quartz was also used for polishing the surface' is a typical entry in the book. A little map that shows the narrow green fertile strip of the Nile is next to a tiny 1880 painting of Nile travellers, with the white outline of the pyramids on the skyline.

So that teachers and pupils can make the most of these resources the publishers have prepared a kit for project work in school. It is skilfully, even elaborately done to promote careful looking and thinking. The learners are encouraged to distinguish between primary and secondary sources by taking on the role of a modern historian and making inferences about finds. This material goes more than part of the way to modify my earlier objections to what is offered to the young for book learning.

Two hesitations remain. With such a richness of resources teachers may never be inclined to question what they can now have as lesson material. But children should always be encouraged to go beyond the information given: first, to wonder how historians know how to bring together the relics and other evidence, and to ask how they came to know what to tell other people about what they discovered.

When I see groups of children in the British Museum standing round the Rosetta Stone, listening to the expert's explanation of why it's important, I wonder if these listeners are told what the writing *says*, that made it necessary to write it three times in different scripts. Are they intrigued by the way it helped to solve the puzzle of the hieroglyphics which had remained a mystery for so long?

Teachers who are satisfied with materials published for examination preparation and believe that these resources need to be neither changed or superseded are not likely to awaken the kind of curiosity that makes history learning exciting. That way lies pedagogic stalemate. Looking and talking, reading and writing still have to include wondering and querying. Even the best books cannot do for the readers the thinking they must do for themselves.

Sometimes readers report about their reading of information books that they remember details that matter to them alone. At the end of my encounters with books about ancient Egypt I found this was the case. Paper and writing were mentioned in nearly every book I read, so I think I know at last how papyrus became a writing surface. The secret is in the sap of the reeds, which glues them together when the strips of the stalk are laid in a frame and pressed down under linen. After that the surface of the matted leaves is rubbed smooth for writing. No single book made all of that clear. My summary is what I pieced together from a number of sources.

Likewise, explorers of the past take from their findings what seems relevant to their own day and age; they cannot entirely discard their contemporary sensibilities. Two things stay with me from this exercise. Learners need to know that 'the facts' may be the same in a number of books, but interpretations of them are

63

likely to be different. Also, it is impossible to treat a historical topic without invoking narrative at some stage, and equally impossible to create a historical narration without moralizing about social life.

Until they are knowledgeable enough to argue about what counts as evidence, what children in school learn about history will depend on who tells them the most memorable stories. This is the curriculum makers' puzzle: whose version of the past is to be believed? Scores of teachers have succeeded in inspiring generations of scholars, just as many have failed to light the slightest flicker of interest or curiosity. The difference lies not in the events or ideas as intrinsically interesting or boring, but in the details and the tone of the telling.

I am returning to the theme which first brought me into contact with books for children: the distinctive nature of historical novels written by authors who took their readers seriously. In 1968 James Moffett, in a book called *Teaching the Universe of Discourse*, argued that, until formal thinking and abstractive categorizing become firmly established in children, narrative has to serve for most kinds of learning. Now we know that Roman Britain was not in every respect exactly as Rosemary Sutcliff represents it in *The Eagle of the Ninth* and *The Lantern Bearers*. But how do you think ten- or eleven-year-olds *envisage* the withdrawal of the Roman legions from Britain and the coming of the Vikings? What, of the former as civilization, could be saved or would survive? Sutcliff knew, from published history, that some Romans stayed behind and some Norsemen were less fierce than others.

Those who want to engage young readers in the topics of history before they can be expected to interpret evidence are not necessarily intellectual weaklings. Novelists, if they are professionally serious, are no less constrained by 'the facts' than historians. They also respect their readers as learners. In return, many young historians have come to understand how they are tied to the long string of the past with the help of novelists like Geoffrey Trease, Rosemary Sutcliff, Hester Burton, Leon Garfield, Barbara Willard, Jill Paton Walsh and others.

To see how this works, look at one of the Mantlemass novels of Barbara Willard. Mantlemass is a manor farm in Ashdown Forest. Its imaginary inhabitants and people in the surrounding villages are caught up in the events of 1485, the end of the Wars of the Roses, until the burning of the house in the Civil War, nearly two centuries later. From these books my pupils discovered what their history texts did not tell them: what it might have been *like* to be a young person in that house and community. They also discovered about early English coal mining, transport in winter, social class as a human problem then as now, loyalties split by family differences, what happened to nuns after the dissolution of the monasteries, as well as just how English is the accepted view of the Armada. In a series like this the novels capture the complexity of a historical moment and show how it can be contextualized in a longer time line, *la longue durée* that Braudel taught us to recognize. Novels may be useless for 'looking up', but 'coming across' things, ideas as well as events, is also an important kind of book learning.

If you find this difficult to believe, read, adultly, *The Name of the Rose*, Umberto Eco's historical detective story. Then, to discover what is going on when you are reading it, turn to Eco's impressively tiny book, *Reflections on 'The Name of the Rose'*, to see how this famous semiotician has made a world model of the Middle Ages in the labyrinth of an imaginary medieval monastery. Eco says there are three ways of narrating the past in fiction: first, as *romance*, 'the past as scenery, pretext, fairy tale construction'. (Science fiction is romance.) The second is 'the swashbuckling novel', cloak-and-dagger stories like *The Three Musketeers*, set in a 'real' and recognizable past with actual historical characters and events as well as fictive ones. Then, there is the historical novel where, Eco says, what the imagined characters do

> serves to make history, what happened, more comprehensible. Events and characters are made up, yet they tell us things about . . . the period that history books have never told us so clearly. (75)

Good novelists have the same passion for detail as social, economic, military and political historians. They also do more with their sources of information, make them count for more. The common purpose is 'to make clearer to us contemporaries what happened then, and how what happened then matters to us as well'. Eco again: 'a historical novelist should not only identify in the past the causes of what came later, but also trace the process through which these causes began to produce their effects.' To do this well is as much the obligation of the topic-book writer as the novelist or the historian.

As long as books for learning are tied to compulsory programmes of study in terms of content and perspective, children learn history as 'what you are given is what you get'. Imagination fades. Proper learning about history extends beyond text, important as text is to bring ideas together. Evidence comes in many forms: buildings, bills of lading, laws, signs, all kinds of writing—including the texts of treaties, insults, religious pronouncements, bonds of peace. Children seem to understand ancient and modern cosmologies more by reading the world-making of novelists and biographers than by memorizing the prose of pedants. Because of the layered nature of language, readers of historical novels come more quickly to the notion that history is a series of versions of the past, not a single telling. Too many history books for young learners are stuck in old modes of writing, for all that they are decorated with the modern means of production. They need to be made anew.

Short, simplified, and selective history books for young readers must be difficult to produce. The decisions taken about what is to be made available, the points of view to be presented, the circumstances of their conception and delivery are rarely discussed in public. How do children, their preoccupations so strongly located in the here and now, learn to look backwards in time, if not from the stories of their elders and phrases like 'before you were born'? What do they learn from commemorations and anniversaries celebrated long after the events they signify? In what circumstances do they see themselves as part of history, or is history always other people?

Teachers have long exerted strong pressure on publishers and others to do away with the exclusions, the partiality, indeed, the racism, of history texts. No more will 'Britannia's Growth and Greatness' do for all children in British schools. Those who do not see their familial past reflected in their schoolbooks must no longer be expected to tolerate only repeated representations of a dominant elite culture. For all the threatening limitations of notions such as 'political correctness', there is now a more informed general understanding of the need for a greater range of 'situated perspectives' in the books we expect children to learn from about the past. But the Englishness of English history dies hard.

School history books have many gaps and different kinds of omissions. Readers whose alignment with the text coincides with that of the writer are less likely to be disturbed by what is written than those who do not begin from the same viewpoint. It took me a long time to realize that I accepted I would read stories written for boys while my brother had never even considered reading one of my library books about girls in boarding schools. Long after I was aware of the absence of working-class children from novels that won the Carnegie Medal for children's literature I was profoundly shaken by Raymond Williams's reading of seventeenth-century poems about country houses. What did they represent for those who built them? Who worked to keep them clean and warm? How were the cleaners paid? Money and power are implicit in most history texts for the young, but these controlling factors rarely surface to be acknowledged until late in book learning.

There are also missing persons: women, mostly, the poor, certainly, as well as 'families of overseas origin' (the phrase used in the 1975 Bullock Report where the needs of bilingual children in British schools were first formally acknowledged), the victims of war, besides those who died in battles, the 'ordinarily' dispossessed. How should we tell children about horrors? One quiet evening, not long before the public events to commemorate World War II, our six-year-old grandson telephoned to ask his grandfather, 'Do you know about Anne Frank?' Without a pause for an answer, at full and detailed length, he related what he had seen on the children's television programme, *Blue Peter*, ending with 'and what do you think of that?' before ringing off. The passion of it dispelled any notion I might have had that history is *simply* text, or *simply* culture.

Slowly, incompletely and, for some, painfully, Europeans are coming to understand the limited perspectives of school history teaching. In Britain some history books still keep alive laudatory accounts of our colonial past, and writers still say that the ancestral homelands of many Britons were 'discovered' by those who sailed from the British Isles. Women's distinctive roles and activities in centuries past are now generally acknowledged, but there is still a hint of special pleading when female examples are brought together in books. Too many accounts still fail to resist stereotypical presentations of national character, as in 'the Irish'. To be sensitive to the histories of the people of Ireland seems an obvious present need, but texts always lag behind events. Persistent acts of unawareness suggest that writers and publishers are still denying that some people *have* a history.

Conscious of gaps in many earlier texts, publishers now commission books that confront 'problems' to bring current events into sharper focus. Thus 'racism', 'unemployment' and 'poverty' are given historical treatment in the same way as 'Aids', 'housing' and 'football' are linked with social studies. *Black and British* by David Bygott, which won the *Times Educational Supplement* Information Book Award for 1992, raises the issues of slavery, exploitation, social unease at immigration numbers, while documenting in detail the slow changes in the laws, and the still slower changes in nationalistic attitudes to Black people.

A simpler book—too simple, perhaps, for its subject—*Let's Talk About Racism* by Angela Grunsell asks topic questions: What is Racism? What is Prejudice? What is a Stereotype? and others in the same vein. Here is part of the text facing the picture of a potential victim of racism. The question is: 'How do I deal with racist insults?'

> Any group can become the target of racism. Feeling good about who you are cannot prevent other people from insulting you, but it can help you to deal with it better. You can learn to avoid some confrontations, by acting with dignity and refusing to let other people annoy you. You may need to judge quite carefully the right moment to stand up for yourself and others, and when to get help, or simply leave a situation quickly. Everyone needs to learn ways of surviving. When people get together to take action against unfair treatment, they can change things. (28)

I doubt that young people who have suffered racial discrimination go first to a book for information about how to confront it. The time lines of this topic are more complex than this paragraph suggests. But the writer confirms the right of the oppressed to be both angry and dignified as part of their understanding of any crass act towards them.

Much of what we learn from history is about survival. Whatever is handed on by each generation contains, in proverbs as well as in public records or autobiographies, the ways our forebears confronted what they feared and relished what they believed was worthwhile. Young people profit from history texts that make past events humanly understandable and offer some insight into present complexities. My disquiet comes from the evidence that history books are now splendid illustrations of the past rather than interpretations of it. The abundance of source material does not always come with help to read it well and critically.

EIGHT

The Body as Metaphor

The conditions of modern social life are, for the most part, what people have in common, what can be shared and seen. Since the beginnings of history, cultural conventions have generally upheld the idea that the bodily parts of our common humanity were to be considered private—withdrawn from common gaze. Lately, this has greatly changed. Now bodily forms and functions are social knowledge, explained, described, explicated, made plain as common-sense conversations about health or common legislation about illness. Yet it is still in our bodies that we locate our private selves, our thoughts and feelings, our sense of individual identity or personality, whatever is unique, different, separate.

Most books about the human body, including those for children at school, are repulsively attractive. As we read them, our hearts pump, our blood flows, we digest food, our eyes and brains assimilate pictures, diagrams and words about our insides—invisible yet felt—as representations on a page. In books our vital organs have names borrowed from distinguished practitioners and from words with Greek roots that recall the history of anatomy and medicine. Cell photography, maps of the nervous system, drawings of intricately related bones, packed layers of muscles and loops of intestines, together with arrowed directions of blood pipes, cross-sections of nails and hair follicles, all startle us as we see our ordinary selves revealed, metaphorically, as cisterns and systems, like plumbing. Yet only inside ourselves does anything actually move. The body in a book is a branch of pathology.

What are young learners discovering about themselves as they look at these close-up stills and interpret these metaphors? Is the knowledge they gather from the naming of parts intellectual, practical or some other kind? I've heard it said that some future doctors take their first steps with school topic books, but the evidence for that is not of the kind that the profession admits. My own experience is of little help. In my school days I saw no such diagrams; 'the

70

body' as a common possession was a secret as well kept as death. Now, children in primary schools can describe digestive and reproductive systems, roughly perhaps, but with straightforward confidence. The human body is no longer a private mystery but simply common sense, especially for advertisers.

Most books for the young present an idealized model of a uniform structure of humans. (Differences are visible only in real people.) Diagrams and drawings are supported by texts which count on the readers' familiarity with their own skin, blood and bones, and also present additional information, aided by similes and metaphors. Intestines are 'brownish red, like meat'. Nails are 'hard skin, something for flesh and bone to press against'. As we might guess, the most interesting parts for a reader making sense of a text in his or her own context are the descriptions of the dark, cold area of the brain. Look carefully at books you read to see if the brain is described as being 'like a computer'.

Ask yourself what you think this means, and if you believe it. To describe the living organism, writers force comparisons with things that people ordinarily recognize or use. Do our bodies 'work' in the sense that we put them to work, or in the other sense of 'how things work'? To reveal to us the parts of ourselves that we may feel but not see, metaphors are probably essential, but some are more confusing than enlightening. All of them betray something of the writers' 'final' vocabularies, the words that compose their view of the world. It is interesting to note how many of the comparisons are linked to recent advances in technology.

What's Inside You? by Susan Meredith is a book that children pore over and talk to each other about. The text has: 'Your brain is connected to all parts of your body by nerves. These are a bit like telephone wires.' Some town-dwelling children ask, 'What are telephone wires like?' Pause to discover who has seen them. At the next question, 'Where is your brain?' they point confidently to their heads. Press on. 'How is your brain connected to your feet?' They look at their wiggling toes. One says, 'The lines are inside the foot', which may mean the child is now considering the possibility that there's an interior string or another kind of attachment. Asked, 'Do you feel your toes?' Yes, they do. They also think that the feeling is in the toes. The text says: 'Your brain makes sense of what happens to you.' This seems to be an acceptable idea, although it doesn't seem to be connected with toes. An older child says, 'If it isn't sensible your brain won't believe it', showing that the mind-brain problem hasn't yet arisen for him. The youngest says, 'My brain's called Bythnia [my invented spelling] and she talks to me.'

This evidence for inner speech indicates, as does his early reading competence, that he knows how to be both the teller and the told. What will he discover that will make him have a different, non-animistic view of his brain? If we read on in this same text we find the sentence: 'There are some parts of the brain that nobody knows much about.' 'Why?' the children ask. The adult explains that nobody, not even the writer of a book, knows everything, but perhaps when they are older they will find out.

Books about the human body rarely satisfy children's curiosity directly. In presenting the parts in an idealized form, writers forget to tell readers that what we know about our bodies in health comes from centuries of study of sickness and disease. Attempts to convey the wondrous intricacies of our insides without the presence of a self means that the heavy load of generalization turns the topic into stodgy reading. The metaphors hint at the limitations, rather than the possibilities, of our make-up: 'job', 'work', 'messages' are not overtures to enlightenment about how our bodies function. Consciousness is never mentioned in the score of books I've read. Statements such as 'the skeleton is wonderfully designed for its purpose' is an example of how pre-Darwinian is much of the explanation. Book versions of human anatomy do not indicate the process of evolution half so forcefully as the skull on the desk in paintings of mediaeval and Renaissance scholars.

Children are never told that we are the only creatures who know about our death, although this was common knowledge to their great-grandparents when young. At best, many 'body' books are prompt copies for talk that moves quickly on to accidents, injuries, illness and sudden death, either in life or on films. We have yet to discover how biology on the page can be made as enlivening as hospital dramas on television.

A book that stands out because it does not conform to any genre is *The Amazing Voyage of the Cucumber Sandwich*. There are no diagrams, only some indifferent zany sketches, but an intriguing text about how whatever we eat turns into us keeps the reader spellbound. Information that in a traditional schoolbook would be conveyed in an impersonal way is here presented in a manner that engages the reader's imagination:

> If you're lucky enough to live in a part of the world where there is plenty of food the total you will eat during your life is likely to weigh over 30,000 kilograms. This would fill about 750 supermarket trolleys. It's equivalent to the weight of six African elephants. On top of that it's also been worked out that you'll drink about 40,000 litres of fluids. An amazing variety of food makes the journey into you through your open mouth. (7)

There then follows the story of the Earl of Sandwich, and how his name became our lunch. The author, Dr Pete Rowan, even includes an idea I've looked for in vain elsewhere: 'There are bound to be exceptions to some of the amazing facts you'll read here about the human body. There isn't such a thing as an "average person". We are all different.'

Have you any idea of the relief such reassurance brings to an adolescent? Think of the success of *The Secret Diary of Adrian Mole aged 13¾*. So in Dr Rowan's next chapter the reader chews the cucumber sandwich and sends it on its way. There follows operation overload: a detailed time line of what a stomach received on Christmas Day, the way in and the way out. Now, examine the metaphors of this paragraph.

> When food arrives, the muscles in the stomach walls churn and mix the meal like a washing machine cleaning clothes or a cement mixer making cement. Glands in the walls add strong acid and other digestive juices. Nothing should be able to get out at this stage. At each end, tight circular muscles like elastic bands keep the mixture in until it is ready to be passed on. (17)

'Nothing should be able to get out at this stage' is the function of the stomach that other descriptions ignore.

Next, we are quickly told of Dr William Beaumont, who was the first person to get a direct glimpse of the interior of the stomach through a partly healed shot wound in the side of Alexis St Martin in 1822. 'Beaumont used to dangle various foods on silk threads into St Martin's stomach to see what happened.' Textual sideslippings and other asides give the readers a notion of the human endeavour such investigations demand, even now, when technology is light years ahead of food on a string. In Rowan's text, as the cucumber sandwich goes on its way through our insides and our understanding, nothing is dehumanized into pipes and machinery. Learning includes wonder.

Memorable phrases about details are this author's specialism. From a later book, *Some Body!*: 'The overall champion for precise movement and sensation is the thumb.' 'Involuntary muscles work by themselves, outside your control. You can hear them working when your heart beats, or your food gurgles on its way through your body.' A baby's acute hearing is linked to the lowest note in a Mozart opera.

This text is more approachable by the young than *The Human Body*, in which Dr Jonathan Miller's staidly dignified prose matches the importance of the enterprise (illustrated with David Pelham's three-dimensional designs) so that the reader feels Science is unrolling its secrets. Young readers are not immediately drawn in by the opening sentence of *The Facts of Life*, by the same expert duo, a feat of paper engineering to match the complexities and details of the subject matter:

> While modern science and technology have made incredible progress in fertilizing techniques occurring outside the female body, the creation and sustenance of early life has not yet been improved by a system more effective than the nurturing of a child in its mother's womb. (1)

Dr Miller's book is a spin-off from a successful TV series where the voice-over coincides with the focus of the pictures presented to viewers. Here again, the immediate facticity of TV outstrips representations in books. You see the heart pumping and the blood flowing. I guess that medical students learn more efficiently from such resources. (Do they still look as carefully as they were once obliged to?) Certainly, their professional context is bound to ensure that the evidence on the screen is linked to hand and eye observation of a genuinely human body.

In books on this topic we see the most definitive changes in social notions about the public and private realms of knowing. There are signs that a wider range of writing and learning styles might progress from popular medical publications on health, sex and disease, to books on topics such as drugs, Aids and socially induced illnesses, designed to be read by the young. If we want children to understand their bodies, books are a help when the writing is not loaded with false and distracting metaphors. We need to rethink this whole topic area. At present our concern to keep the young away from experiences and substances that do them harm also encourages them to dare and be dared, to experiment and experience as ways of challenging themselves and their elders.

The significant feature of young bodies is their rate of change. Most books have diagrams to illustrate increase in body size and the evolution of sex organs, but the texts say little or nothing about accompanying feelings of self-awareness, awkwardness, ambiguity, dread, even. Very little sympathetic understanding is conveyed in schoolbooks when the topic is to be regarded 'scientifically'. The affective side of growing up is left to writing in magazines and novels. For the young their bodies are metaphors of their expectations of life, what they will become, but they find little recognition of this most important 'fact' and scant naming of it in the books they are given to learn from.

The glaring example is in books about human reproduction and sexual behaviour. Parents' anxieties about 'sex education' reflect a more general need to know how books advance learning in both 'facts' and 'feelings'. A Swedish colleague, a critic of books for the young, told me that in her culture sex is regarded as 'important but ordinary'. It could therefore be ordinarily part of books for quite young children as well as those for adolescents. American and British presentation, on film and television especially, confounds learning about health, safety and the care of children with cultural taboos and the breaking of accepted norms of behaviour. Older readers are expected to make sense of formal presentations of human biology in book diagrams modelled on anatomical drawings, while much of what they have already learned comes from oral traditions of common knowledge. Only skilled teachers avoid embarrassment in classroom discussions on these topics. Younger pupils, encouraged to be scrupulous about personal hygiene, are offered books about teeth, hair and diet. Sometimes they are given explanations about changes in their appearance. But a book such as Babette Cole's *Mummy Laid an Egg* is unlikely to be selected by a book club, for all its admirable directness, artistry and subtle humour, before a trial run in a nursery school. Explicitness about bodily functions hovers on the threshold of taboo.

In trying to discover what promotes learning in body books for the young, I found very few instances, and in these only glimpses, of what it is to be human, to be able to regard oneself. No description of how we are showed how we wear out. Topic books about harmful substances and habits explain the dangers, but without any implicit acknowledgement of why or how these things come to be attractive. Overtones of disapproval in the writing crowd out the best intentions of the communicators. Again, emphasis and information overload can be cognitively counterproductive.

About metaphors. This topic context lets us see their importance in learning more generally. In learners, metaphors join the new to the unknown. (Stories do this for young children when most of their learning lies ahead of them.) Most information-book writers try to link new details of systems, events and processes to what they assume is the learners' 'prior knowledge', a phrase now much in vogue, which generally means the popular culture. Metaphors also carry visual and emotional emphases, together with a tonal quality that indicates the relevance or surprise of the new information. Here are examples from *Some Body!* where cells are first described as 'building blocks':

> Not all cells are the same. Like the bricks, tiles and panes of glass that go to make up a house, so the different cells—of bone, skin, blood and fat—go to make up your body. (6)

In the same text we are told that 'the busiest area of the cell is the endoplasmic reticulum'. (An arrow points to the magnified illustration.) 'It is like the industrial complex of a town. Within it are "factories"— called ribosomes.' This metaphor carries on to link the whole process together. The 'greatest delivery service systems in the cell are the vacuoles which move and transport material both within the cell and in and out of the cell.' The 'largest storage depot is the Golgi complex. Protein is stored here until the cell needs it.' The 'most upwardly mobile cell is the male sperm.' This joining of cell descriptions to social systems depends on the illustrations, which show enlarged photographs of cells, but the understanding of the workings is taken from industrial enterprises. The metaphor that lurks in the word 'cell' is also explained: 'The first "cells" seen were not what we know as cells at all, but holes in dead wood. They were called "cells" in 1665 when the

English scientist Robert Hooke used one of the first microscopes to look at thin slices of cork. The cork showed regular small oblong holes so he called them cells because they looked like small rooms.'

Metaphors help thinking; they also renew language, so language and thought extend each other. This efficiency is at its most powerful in continuous texts where it includes and promotes feelings *about* the topic.

NINE

The Idea Behind It

The most challenging topic books I read were about astronomy. Of these, the most remarkable were in a series about the planets, made up from satellite photographs which offered glimpses of outer space hitherto unseen and unrealized. As best I could I used the accompanying text to make sense of what I saw, but was almost entirely at a loss. The world-picture, the cosmology on which the explanations depended, is not part of my understanding. I lacked the idea of 'outer space' which lies behind it.

However, I'm not entirely blank in this area. In the first lesson about Chaucer my literature teacher taught the class how the days of the week came in their particular order and explained why this understanding related to what we were about to read. Someone else explained that Galileo's intellectual feat was not simply his insistence that the earth moved, but that he had imagined what the earth would look like if he were standing on the moon. To grasp what lies beyond our seeing and feeling, it is not information we need first, but conceptions, ideas, including hunches, informal and formal arguments and theories, shot through with imaginative what-ifs. Observations and documentations have to be transformed into ideas, or to be consequent on them for learning to be effective. Information, as Gregory Bateson says, is useful as 'the difference that makes the difference'.

Here is another powerful idea, a signpost for those concerned about children's thinking as the essential part of their book learning. It comes from Vygotsky, whose writings did not become widely known until a long time after his early death in Russia in 1934. Now his ideas about the growth of children's imagination, thought and language are universally discussed and recognized. Vygotsky maintains that all learning is dialogic, like a conversation. It occurs twice: first in the social exchanges of talk and shared activities, especially of adults and children, and then, internally, as 'inner speech' or thinking, as the learner makes the learning *mean.*

Adults, as tellers and talkers, readers and writers, interpret the ways of the world to children in gestures, language, play and books. A book is special as it holds the reader's or listener's thinking at an in-between space where talk-thinking in the world gradually becomes thought-thinking in the head. Book learning is never a simple transference of text to memory, as we have seen. Meaning has to be ascribed by the learner both to the text-in-book context and also to the difference the word meanings make to the reader's view of the world in thought. Just how this sequencing works is what psychologists, brain people and others argue about. But no learning simply occurs; we make it make a difference to the way we think.

Most of the books children are offered at school—textbooks, course books and topic books—are limited by their mundane subject matters. Writers and publishers of new versions of traditional lesson-stuff simply use new designs to attract new learners. Many books reappear with only superficial changes; others just fade away. Lists of titles go out of date, but in school the topics linger on.

Books not directly linked to school learning spring from ideas that writers and designers want to communicate, demonstrate, celebrate, or experiment with in terms of what a book makes possible. The advantage of the book format is that complex systems can be displayed on a well-ordered page so that the intricacies of an idea can be admired together with the aesthetics of the design.

Time and space are two subjects that demand books fired by such 'ideas' people and that provoke the kind of learning Vygotsky describes. When children begin to 'tell the time', where telling means counting as well as saying, they are entering a subject complicated by relativity.

Time is a popular topic in books of learning. There are design possibilities in illustrations of watches and clocks, contrasting pictures of night, day, the seasons, whether in wordless picture books or in those which explain time zones, calendars, pre-mechanical chronometers and digital displays. Here are typical beginnings.

If you had been alive before clocks and watches were invented, you would have learned to tell the time by looking at the position of the Sun in the sky. (Brenda Walpole, *Time*, 4)

79

Before there were clocks and watches, people used the shadows of trees and stones to tell the time. When cities were built, people used the shadows cast by a tower in the town square in the same way. (Mitsumasa Anno, *The Earth is a Sundial*, 6)

These are rational adult starting places, but not very easy for a young person who is preoccupied with a new watch. I am content with a neat note by Marie Heinst, the mathematics consultant for *My First Book of Time* by Claire Llewellyn, to remind parents that children cannot see or feel time. 'The same period seems to pass quickly or slowly, depending on what activity they are engaged in.' This book distinguishes 'telling' the time from 'a sense' of time. Use this idea to differentiate the understandings offered by any other time book that comes your way and remember, 'the age at which children begin to tell the time with any confidence varies enormously'. This is, in fact, a good example of how real learning 'takes' time.

The pictures in Llewellyn's book set time in ordinary human contexts: day and night, a day's events, the days of the week, months, calendar months and making a calendar. This book scores in the variety and flexibility of what it offers to the beginner, an example that could be followed in other topics. It confirms, holds and extends what adults try to make plain to children so that they don't have to take in too much at once.

The idea behind it all is that by learning to tell the time, children can begin to grasp part of one of the most complicated systems that define the world. If they have sorted out a bit of it, they feel independent when they use the words that confirm their existence in time, as yesterday, tomorrow, later, sooner. Then they associate dates with birthdays, a big step if you are five and entering one of the learning dialogues, in the world and in the head, that go on all the time. School is governed by time and timing: classes go up in years, there are time-tables, playtime, timed tests and other ways of marking the passage of what my grandfather called the Old Enemy.

Every day adds something to children's understanding of this central puzzle. Book learning helps to sort out the meanings of time, but, like any other learning, it has to begin where, in time, they are.

*

Space, as both time and distance, is difficult for children to grasp at once, and I am still not sure that books help them to capture not just the facts but the wonder and the mystery of the universe. Most of the books I read on astronomy, even those with the latest photographs, need the accompaniment of a teacher, a telescope or a friend in an observatory. Beginners can learn about space from accounts of actual space travel, which have the tension and drama of the best story adventures into the unknown, not least because the events are outside the actual and possible experience of all but a few. The act of reading, however, even in a bald text, makes the events a virtual experience for children whose mental picture of the universe will be constructed differently from that of their grandparents.

Readers who grew up with Patrick Moore's books about the planets and the stars are probably able to offer reasonable explanations to their children or pupils about the data and details of space. Children who watch sky programmes on television are likely to be familiar with visual presentations of these topics. Books seem to be at their weakest in attempting explanations related to time and space. Good videos are surely the best starting place for young astronomers. Then it's the writers of the accompanying pamphlet who are challenged to describe what the viewer is expected to see and remember, and to explain how the images of infinite space become knowledge.

In the realm of ideas, the names of writers of information books are rarely the shorthand for their contents: the titles are not often best sellers. David Macaulay is the exception. As an Englishman living in North America he has the admiration of both readerships. His conviction about book learning is that 'if you talk about things and illustrate them in a direct, straightforward way then there is no reason why a nine-year-old and a fifty-year-old aren't both going to get something out of the book'. As a writer and an artist, Macaulay has insight, both direct and complex, into how readers can learn by entering the intellectual space where imagination does its work.

Macaulay's reputation for diagrammatic and explicatory clarity began with his earlier books: *Castle*, *Cathedral*, *City*, *Pyramid*. In these he tells and shows how complicated constructions were conceived, crafted and completed when technology, although primitive by today's standards, was effectively adapted to its use. In the fine details of his drawings, he shows how, at each stage of construction, builders and stonemasons exploited to the limit the essential nature of their materials and, in so doing, extended their skill and their craft. Macaulay does this too. The buildings he chooses to represent were, in their beginnings, projects of vision. They often took more than one lifetime to complete.

Among the many forceful ideas that underpin these books is a strong sense of time committed to an ideal. As inheritance, Macaulay assumes the skill of those whose work he celebrates. With imaginative fire he pulls readers in so that they see what the builders have in mind as they flatten the ground in order to begin construction.

In *Cathedral* the dream takes shape in plans for pillars, drawings for carvings and carpentry, in wood, stone, lead and glass. As Macaulay draws his own plans, the reader sees the cathedral growing *up*, skywards. In the words and the pictures the building grows as near as the author can make it to the work of the masons, blacksmiths and builders, whose insights into what the whole building should look like gradually become visible. Thus the book shows the reader the journey from concept to actuality.

Look at the page that demonstrates how the spire was built, and you discover architecture as a way of describing, as well as enclosing, space. By showing his readers the interior ribcage, Macaulay lets them into the secrets of what they would not see as visitors to the completed building. He also evokes the aspiration, the breathing time, of those who wrought the bosses and left on them the faces of their friends and enemies as decorations.

Cathedral is entwined in my reading of an early novel by William Mayne, *Cathedral Wednesday*, and William Golding's *The Spire*. Here is Macaulay's spelling out for his readers the ideas and humane concerns which lie behind his work. 'Although the people of Chutreaux are imaginary, their single-mindedness and their incredible courage are typical of the twelfth, thirteenth and fourteen centuries in Europe where magnificent dreams still stand today.'

Macaulay's masterpiece, *The Way Things Work*, has, since its appearance in 1988, won unlimited, well-deserved praise for all aspects of its excellence. There are 384 large pages of clear, intricate diagrams, illustrations and sprightly text to explain to readers how a number of human inventions, embodying general scientific principles, actually function. It is a rich source of satisfactory explanations in depth not possible in books of lesser status and production. The mechanics of movement, the harnessing of the elements, waves, electricity, automation are all part of our everyday lives. But those of us who are content to let things work until they break down are skimping modern understandings and being less than fair to the ingenuity of the people who devised the machines. Macaulay and his colleagues reveal the workings and insist that readers should understand the principle of how technology makes a difference.

No one who knows how to make things work and can enunciate the scientific ordering of them has acquired these understandings only by reading texts and looking at pictures and diagrams. Hands-on experience is necessary. But many key concepts are the result of mental work, the generalized knowing that comes as the result of seeing that different problems may be solved by invoking the same principle.

Macaulay trusts narrative to explain ideas, and has invented a character, the Woolly Mammoth, who wanders along the edges and sometimes into the pages of this series of scientific explanations. The story exploits of this amiable monster provide memorable instances of the principle underlying a series of mechanical operations. The chapter on Friction begins with 'On Mammoths and Bathing':

> The bathing scene I remember most vividly was not unlike the weighing of a large mammoth in its communal atmosphere. A large sneaker-clad crowd gathered on one side of a bath filled with soap suds. A dirty mammoth sat defiantly on the other. It should be noted that the mammoth's weight is its greatest defence and just by standing or sitting still, it is able to resist all but the most determined efforts to move it.
>
> Once ropes had been attached to the animal, they were pulled tight. Meanwhile, another team used a technique I had not previously encountered in my researches. First, they employed second-class levers [these have been already explained] to raise the beast slightly. Just when I had concluded that they intended to lever it all the way to the tub, some of their number poured a mixture of liquid soap and marbles between the protesting creature and the floor.
>
> The result was astonishing; the animal's resistance was suddenly reduced, and despite its struggles it was hauled inexorably towards the water. Working simultaneously from both ends, it took little more than

half an hour to get the mammoth close enough to the foam-filled tub for a good scrub behind the ears.

Here the style is a parody of classical essay-writing on scientific subjects. The memorable anecdote lets the reader understand the next bit of text: 'friction appears whenever one substance rubs against another, or when an object moves through any other liquid or gas. Friction happens because two surfaces in close contact grip each other. So the gripping has sometimes to be reduced, and at other times to be used, as in car brakes.' The implications extend to oil rigs and also to the impossibility of perpetual motion on earth compared with the free movement of bodies gyrating in space.

Macaulay's narratives include the history of ideas. The Greeks are credited with the earliest notions of elements and atoms. The Chinese had a differential in the third century AD. Locks existed in ancient Egypt. The parachute was forecast by Leonardo da Vinci, and the combine harvester 'makes use of several augers that work exactly in the same way as Archimedes' screws'.

The showing tone of the text conveys the author's wonder and pleasure at human inventiveness. Once you have read his appreciation of the great ingenuity of a sewing machine you feel the same about the book itself. It has been made as Auden made his imaginary leadmine, as the children I know helped their ingenious father to construct a model water mill in transparent plastic so that they would see exactly how the water made the wheels go round. One condition of the imagination is a questing intellect; not an exclusive talent, but potential in all learners, although still unrealized in too few.

Throughout the many pages of *The Way Things Work* I feel I am being properly invited to exercise and to appreciate human understanding. This feeling cannot happen to children too early. Although those now in school are likely to see this book first in its CD-ROM version—where the machines actually do move—I hope that they will have a chance to understand how the book works, for this is no less amazing.

Books that spring from ideas prompt their readers to see beyond the external features of what they are shown. The books I have briefly touched on in this section are attempts to involve readers in understanding the complexity of the relation of ideas to accomplishment, to rouse more questions, even in the youngest child learning to tell the time. They indicate how people are driven to understand more, often by hard effort.

The most useful books invite children to try things out. Those for older children provide quick access to a variety of examples of the construct to be acquired. Sadly, very few books take account of how failure, false starts, incomplete understandings, tentative explorations can be useful ways of discovering the *deliberateness* of learning. (That's where teachers come in.) Tentative explorations are often useful ways of discovering the *deliberateness* of the kind of inquiries we call 'research' and often invite young people to try on their own as a form of explorative learning.

By this time it must be evident that I believe ideas are the important things to be grasped. Information, mostly a spin-off from ideas, has to be located, or, more often, relocated as part of a pattern in the mind of the learner. Information detached from ideas cannot count as knowledge or understanding. In too many books, bits of information are presented by the communicator as something without origins or consequences. In the only books that matter, the writer creates a text in order to conduct a dialogue with the reader about ideas that make a difference. As part of the idea, information then acts like cells in the body, the building blocks of knowing and understanding. The next chapter continues the theme of ideas, this time in relation to what we think of as 'convictions'.

TEN

Moral Imperatives

It is not difficult for adults to understand that the world their children inhabit is different from the one they themselves knew in childhood. We have only to remember what schools, cars, songs, household equipment and television were like 'then', or, in my case, what happened 'before the war', to see social differences. Shifts in shared social understanding—the nature of a family or a community, the obligations of religious adherence, notions of tolerance, conformity and what is to be believed—are less tangible and more likely to emerge as arguments when children prefer the world views of their peers to those of their parents.

If I had any global awareness before I was ten, it was very local. There were certain fixities: Sunday was different from Saturday. When I was in school, male adults went out to work but mothers stayed at home. I was located and defined by my address, which extended to Fife (the county), Scotland (the country), Great Britain (the pink shape on the wall map), Europe (the whole map). I wrote this in the front of a notebook, then a wiser friend told me to add 'The Northern Hemisphere' and 'The Universe', but I was unsure about their location. I knew about Africa, as an uncle was a trader in Nigeria. He told me about 'the slaves'. My parents had friends who were missionaries, so news came from India. Refugees, described as 'the oppressed', were transient guests in the house of my grandparents after 1937, but little emerged then, in my hearing, about their more general plight. I knew they were Jews, without any understanding of what that implied.

Personal knowledge of emotions, illness, diet, social and sexual behaviour, the rights of women, unemployment (locally called 'being idle'), and most moral imperatives depended for their interpretation on the authority of my elders. I now know that I had a less rigorously gendered view of what the future offered than that of my schoolfriends. Nowadays, young readers can find books on most of these topics. Until full adolescence I had no idea they could be written about as 'issues'.

When I told my children about my early intuitions, uncorrected until dangerously late, about how any living species reproduced itself, their response was incredulous hilarity. To encounter the shock of adolescent growth and change, not a single text was within my reach. A picture book such as Babette Cole's *Mummy Laid an Egg* (published in 1994), in which two very young children undertake, by drawing pictures, to dispel what they think is their parents' ignorance of conception and birth, was not only unavailable; it was unimaginable. I knew nothing about dinosaurs. Science, as explanations of the 'real' world, came after I had memorized a list of chemical formulae. From sermons I had learned words like evil, sin, righteousness, compassion, wisdom (and, of course, meekness, which was embarrassing). I had no idea that the world might be affected by anything I did or thought.

As they learn their language in conversation with their elders, children learn their culture, including its values and taboos, its facts and fantasies, as their first picture of the world. Today, their global locality is no longer an address but a series of visual images of the universe. Before they leave primary school they understand that they are seeing world events as they occur. Growth and changes, which in actuality take months or years, are presented as a ten-minute narrative on television. A foetus, for millennia invisible, becomes a child before their very eyes. Geography includes a direct vision of polar regions. Gone are the drawings in books of huskies and tents. Instead, explorers are winched to helicopters from icefloes while voice-overs describe the event. Close-ups of Amazon forests, transcontinental train rides, space walkers on interstellar platforms are all part of their vocabulary as well as virtual experiences. With these changes come others, in what young people *imagine* the world is like, and what is important about it.

The subtle changes in the shared cultural framework of different generations also surround the prescriptive conventions of moral behaviour: what counts as a principle (about stealing, deceit, winning, succeeding) or justification, or certain kinds of obligation, and the 'oughts' of everyday encounters. Piaget explored some of the early stages in the development of morals by watching boys playing marbles, learning what counted as the rules and how to win without cheating. Nowadays morality is widely discussed in relation to events reported by the media. How do parents explain a 'serial killer'? Are wars inevitable? When is collaboration better than competition? How do we know what is fair? 'Setting an example'—a constant preoccupation of the class-conscious Victorians—no longer prevails.

And yet, the history of children's books shows that, in every age, the didactic intent is not far from most texts. The implication of what counts as normative behaviour underlies all storytelling. Sometimes this is made explicit; more often it lurks beneath the surface of what adults expect children to understand. Although we are a long way from the 'goodly godly' books of the seventeenth century, we might be nearer than is generally acknowledged to their awareness that a belief is an emotion as well as an argument. Here are some examples of books where moral imperatives are more or less obvious. The question for adult readers is, do they, the books, help young people to understand themselves, their social world and other people better so as to make more considered judgements when more than one point of view is presented?

In response to an obvious need to portray in books the multicultural nature of Western countries, especially in cities, most information book publishers have series about world religions. A typical example is Lynn Underwood's *Religions of the World*, which presents the main religions, including tribal rites, in terms of traditional belief, important incidents or people and modern practices. The pictures are dominant, the statements clear to those who have already some inkling of the topic, baffling for others. The section on 'Religions Today' raises important questions about tolerance, multiculturalism and the coexistence of people of different faiths. The usefulness of a book like this depends on what additional documentation is available for the learners and how open are the discussions provoked by the ideas in it. Every religious denomination has its own holy book, in which good behaviour is codified. There are also privileged readings of these. The blandness of an over-generalized text conceals the existence, and the dangers, of fundamentalism.

Most books about religions are well-intentioned in their explanations about differences, somewhat over-anxious to be even-handed in some cases. But none gives any notion of why people are willing to commit atrocities and to die for what they believe. The lack of informed writing about these books and of critical discrimination among them is very striking.

Books about diverse faiths have an implied, rarely discussed notion of tolerance. Few readers are aware that it is not a universal understanding. Who tolerates whom? We could know more about how children transform their cultural awareness and their learning from books into patterns of behaviour and a moral code if we discovered how they come to empathize with others and to see an event or a conviction from another viewpoint.

Family, and community, then school, expect conformist behaviours. Various kinds of pressure, the 'oughts', come to children as feelings before they can judge for themselves the rightness and wrongness of a set of propositions about human knowledge and behaviour. When do they learn about dissent?

It is not difficult to engage the sympathies of young people for good causes. Most schools have charity collections as part of endeavours to promote social awareness. Without the efforts of the young such global feats as 'Band Aid' and 'Help' would be less successful. Young children are spontaneous in their responses to injustice, cruelty, loss and deprivation, which they now see on a world scale. There has even been some suggestion that they may suffer, intermittently at least, from 'compassion fatigue'.

Social problems addressed in books of information are designed to extend the readers' empathy to the plight of other people. Some of the concerns may be personal and local: bullying in school, for example. Others arise in multinational contexts: famine, poverty, disease, ecological distress, refugees, where groups of people are threatened or at the mercy of the more powerful. Racism, both local and international, shows that 'issues' arise in conditions governed by notions of difference, the others-are-not-like-us syndrome, which involves everyone. Consider gender. Most teachers are aware of distinctive differences in the learning styles of boys and girls as they progress through school, but many do not know how to help young people to understand these things in themselves as they become aware of the nature of differing sexual orientations. Writers of information books are inclined to assume that their books will be read by boys, but rarely say so.

I have been greatly struck by the impression that the conventional format of many books of information actually prevents complex problems from being explored. The issues are soundly 'raised' and exemplified, but in most cases there is little discussion, perhaps on the ground that children have too little experience to bring to the texts. If we consider books which discuss bullying, currently regarded as one of the social hazards of school, we might see if the open discussion of it makes it less threatening than the silent fear endured by many children who are ill-treated physically and verbally. Two books on the topic are: Karen Bryant-Mole's *What's Happening? Bullying* and Pete Saunders's *What do you know about bullying?* The emphasis in both of these books is on understanding the social nature of the problem, the weakness of the bully and the need to persuade the victim to seek adult help undeterred by the stigma of 'telling tales', but neither book has the complexity and felt life of Aidan Chambers's story, *The Present Takers*, where the reader has to face what the characters fear and endure.

Here, again, I am persuaded that the best books for the young about moral issues are novels where the author can explore a range of feelings, meanings and intentions from different points of view in ways that bring the reader close to characters, events and decision-making. In these books of non-fiction, the narrative has only a spurious reality. Consider wars. School lessons for pupils in middle childhood recount the events and outcomes in many contexts, without making a direct link between bullying and war in terms of moral imperatives. As with the issue of human rights, the abstract concept has to be firmly located in specific examples, and books on these subjects inevitably date very quickly.

Books for learning carry implicit as well as explicit messages that are part of larger cultural understandings, both the dominant versions and those associated with dissent. Reading sets up an internal dialogue in readers between what they are coming to know and what they have hitherto assumed to be the case. When they begin to explore topics of powerful social concern to adults, young people sometimes feel uneasy in ways that they cannot, or are unwilling, to explain. Books which offer them most scope to examine what they think also give them a chance to enter into a kind of dialogue with the author in the act of reading, and into dialogue with themselves thereafter.

The development of readers is no less complex than their development as human beings. In both cases they 'grow into rules', often painfully when they try to understand complicated ideas. To what they learn as 'facts' from authoritative texts they attribute the necessity of belief, so there are often periods of confusion. Here are some examples of intellectual understandings which sometimes appear as moral imperatives in books designed to teach what is now known about the world.

As an example of shared popular assumptions about what we believe science tells us, think about dinosaurs, and about what adults and children believe about these creatures. There seem to be more books about dinosaurs than any other topic. As a school centre of interest they hover between what young people come to recognize as science and what is split off as imagination, a caesura that characterizes much of their later formal study. Theories are the meeting place of evidence and imagination. It is helpful, therefore, in reading dinosaur books to examine the boundaries of what the writers suggest is 'true' and what kind of credence he or she expects from readers.

Adults divide their belief in dinosaurs in the same way as children. On the one hand, palaeontological research comes from different kinds of fieldwork and different interpretations of what counts as evidence. The DNA of extinct animals can be produced from fossil material, and there are ways of linking this with living organisms. In writing about how we know about dinosaurs, Brian Rosen of the Museum of Natural History says,

> A time-honoured treatment of fossil remains puts them into an over-all evolutionary narrative. Such evolutionary narratives are presented as some kind of scientifically factual 'truth', but are actually constructs linking together apparently related living and fossil organisms.

This linking-to-make-a-narrative interests me because, in children's learning from books, scientific truth comes with a moral imperative to be believed. On the other hand, however, adults as well as children fill the gaps in their understanding of the beginning of things with monsters in films like *Jurassic Park*.

Most seven- to nine-year-olds have a favourite dinosaur book, especially boys. (My guess is that here the male concern with the way things really are still clings to the imaginative possibilities of the monsters.) Readers say that they look for 'all the facts'. They use a dinosaur encyclopaedia and read *The Ultimate Dinosaur Book*, written by David Lambert and approved by the Museum of

Natural History. They believe dinosaurs were real.

Perhaps dinosaurs score by being the topic where imagination and fact count equally in learning from books. We have to imagine evolution, even when TV and CD-ROM make movement for us to watch. The rise and fall of dinosaurs is learned from the narrative that gives the story a time line.

The young readers I know treat the creatures as characters with exotic names. They make imaginative fictions from the book illustrations of limitless swamps and plains that accompany the detailed drawings of the dinosaurs' distinguishing features. They deliberate about different kinds of dinosaur food and have theories about why they disappeared. The explanation which emphasizes a celestial bombardment of meteorites and asteroids has won favour. This is a world as imaginary, and therefore as real, as any other landscape with clashing warriors and mythic beasts. Even very young readers discover the central 'fact' about dinosaurs in a picture book, *Dinosaurs and All That Rubbish*, by Michael Foreman. With their great feet, the one thing we really do know about, these story dinosaurs pound down all the rubbish tips around them to make the world green again. For both children and adults dinosaurs are metaphors for what we apprehend in a rapidly changing world we only partly comprehend.

Most British children understand and are frightened by cruelty to animals. The topic has a particular cultural resonance. It also has a long history in children's story books. Now the focus is on the animals that have become rare and are threatened with extinction. Special interest groups have come together to become a movement by urging their concern on others. Gone are the days, and the books, when the beasts of Africa were a challenge to experts with guns and trapping equipment. Although Disney's *The Lion King* successfully invokes notions of 'nobility', the heads of horned beasts no longer decorate walls; piano keys are plastic not tusk ivory; fur coats provoke outrage. To visit a zoo is to recognize that concern has replaced collection.

Television films have made exotic animals familiar in their own habitats and promoted the idea that each of us has an individual responsibility for the conservation of both ordinary and endangered species. The book-learning aspect of this kind of concern, sometimes domestic, as in the case of transporting calves to other countries to be killed for food, or sometimes global, the over-fishing of the seas, lets us see how children become first interested and then involved in topics where their feelings are directly engaged. Again, I contrast my experience with theirs.

When I was eleven I saw a beached whale. The circumstances are now vague, but I remember people said it was an accident. The size, texture and inertness of the beast—it was crumpled, dirty and looked old—produced a mixture of fear and repugnance. I had no concern for its plight. I had learned that Eskimos ate blubber, but beyond that, I was disinclined to be curious. I think the notion of blubber, the very sound of the word, was queasy-making. Many years later when I read *Moby Dick* and swam through that swelling prose, caught up in Captain Ahab's obsessive chase, I came to believe that I knew whales intimately, yet, at that time, I had no recollection of the one I had seen hanging by its tail fin.

Now children are told that whales are an endangered species and have to be saved from extinction. Commitment to knowledge is not enough; there has to be responsibility for the creatures, so children's sympathy for good causes is enlisted as they learn. By tapping into their concern, teachers hope to extend their span of attention to the topic. 'What *shall* we do about the whales?' a child suddenly asked at bedtime a propos of nothing we had just been discussing.

There is a fine line between learning about whales and being overwhelmed by the need to care for them. Perhaps we should inspect more closely the imperative rhetoric of general obligation and ask what part it plays in modern book learning. Here is a book that makes no bones about its emphasis: *The Blue Whale* by Melissa Kim, illustrated by Shirley Felts. It sets out its moral purpose on the first page, headed 'The whales need you!'

The blue whale: the biggest, most magnificent creature ever to grace the earth has been endangered for many years. Why? Man hunted the blue whales until there were very few left.

If we look at the blue whale and its plight, we can understand more about whales and perhaps help to preserve the other species of whales that are still in danger—before it's too late and all the great mammals of the sea are only pictures in a book.

If you care about animals in danger you automatically become a Wildlifer. Wildlifers are just people who share a common concern for

animals and want to do something to make the world a better place for
the blue whale and for all of us. (3)

All books for children, not only those designed for their learning, are imbued with the author's didactic intents. In information
texts these are more up front. Where a strong desire to engage children's interests is overlaid with too urgent pleading, messages
about ecology and saving the planet seem destined to fulfil the
same purposes as those of nineteenth-century Sunday school tracts,
or of later scripture lessons about being good. Fundamentalist
devotion to a single viewpoint, or to the imposition of a range of
social taboos, is not confined to religious affairs.

Consider the number of recent information books for the
young about rainforests, another popular classroom topic in the
newer studies associated with geography. The issues are more complex than they appear in the short texts of information books. Like
whales and seals, rainforests are the basis of the economy in more
than one country. What for one group is a moral crusade, for
another is a threat to its livelihood. Very few books for young
people about rainforests explore the nature of conflicting interests
in any depth.

The hardest thing to find in books about the rainforests is a
straightforward description and presentation of the ecosystem in
ways that let the feelings of the readers become involved without
guilt. Some texts veer towards romantic excess: 'The forest stirred;
Taca heard the message with deep foreboding . . . ' Others offer a
kind of equatorial pastoral. In *Brunei Rainforest Adventure* three
teenagers, a writer, a musician and an artist, are chosen to visit the
Batu Apoi Forest Reserve to see how the forests are being re-
claimed and put to more use than they would be when cut up as
logs. The fine photographs are of a television quality, but some
seem to have the self-conscious posing of holiday snaps, perhaps
intentionally. The involvement of the visitors appears superficial,
until one reads what they wrote, movingly, about their experiences
and the changes of their perspectives on the world. For young readers this point is lost because the ecological emphasis on rural re-
demption is further confused by travelogue prose, and the 'having
a great time'-ness of the pictures. Yet this book is seriously meant.
It addresses the results of carefully won knowledge applied to
threatened areas full of natural resources. To discover this, the

94

reader has to understand that the words of the text go more deeply into the purpose of the visit than the pictures do.

On the whole, books about rainforests are single-issue texts. The productions are thickened with advice on how the individual reader can become a member of a pressure group. Mission statements are made in question form such as, 'Do you like chocolate?' followed by 'Then you should know that areas of forest are being developed for cash crops such as cocoa, and the animals, whose natural habitat this is, are being forced to leave.' Or, 'Look in your local pet shop to see if the parrot cages are big enough.' Young readers want to be associated with moves to save the planet, but sometimes, in reading about what they should do, they are overwhelmed by feelings of inadequacy. More significantly than television, books could help them to develop an understanding of the delicate balancing act of preserving and using the earth's resources, especially if the writers explained the problems in ways which helped their readers to deal with some of the complexities.

Somewhat dispirited by encounters with rainforest texts, I went with a young friend, at his request, on his first visit to Kew. He chose to see the carnivorous plants, a good plunge into the exotic heat of a greenhouse and a chance for him to expand my understanding of the 'greenhouse effect'. Once in the great Palm House, we were surrounded by the drama of the rainforest. No need here to urge the pliant splendour of tall bamboos, prolific palms, teak as a real tree, succulent greenery and all the fragrance of that wet steaminess. It was a new experience for my companion, one of the world's glories. Here the desire to preserve the rainforest came from the beauty of the plants themselves, beyond any moral urging.

It is helpful for the young to discover that facts are many-faceted, that engagement with them involves acts of critical reading, when the reader has to ask, as I have said so often, 'who says?' 'who sees?' Too much emphasis on making books visually attractive has led to some noticeable over-simplification of serious subjects. Yet, paradoxically, even some superficial texts generate in young people the idealism necessary to approach world problems. The important intellectual discovery is that effective action in these domains must be based on accurate knowledge and critical judgement. Book learning is as necessary as practical experience; each must complement and extend the other.

The beginnings of social morality are nearer to home than the rainforests, in responsibility for local environments. When I was young, rubbish was collected by a man with a cart on Thursdays. Most lemonade bottles were re-used for paraffin or exchanged at shops for pennies. In wartime, recycled paper was a necessity, not a sign of ecological correctness. Now we *do* waste too much, and to teach young people not to be extravagant with the earth's resources is necessary and good sense. They also need to be aware of some of the known health hazards of modern living which may affect them before the rising of the seas, but it is difficult to present in every book the threat of nuclear fuel storage and food additives. Advertisers know about over-emphasis; constant reminders about cholesterol, alcohol, smoking and air pollution sometimes make little impact. We know we should alert each other to the risks of pollen counts and sunbathing, but we don't want to spoil one another's enjoyment in doing so.

The communicative task faced by writers, designers and publishers of books on topics that generate moral imperatives is not simply that of using language and pictorial representations to make the facts comprehensible. Rather it is to imagine how their readers will make sense of them. How do they interpret new ideas and information in terms of what they already know? Very few writers have enough space in information books to *explore* what might be taken for granted about a subject so as to introduce new information to *extend* the readers' knowing. Even topics as apparently straightforward as 'beans' or 'rubbish' need word space. A world of objects has to be represented in language, signs or pictures, before it can be argued about. We know how even the best texts can be misunderstood.

I have had to be a learner in all of this, which is why there are no conclusions. Children and their teachers, talking together about something they have read, *The Life of Mary Seacole* or *The Diary of Anne Frank*, have shown me how tentative explorations are often better for understanding than unexamined assumptions or didactic insistence. When the *fatwa* was first pronounced on Salman Rushdie, the native-born pupils in a London class demanded that their quiet Muslim friend should explain what it meant. He did so, with a dignified expertise that surprised them. The ensuing discussion had more significance, more acute demands for sources of information, more moral sway than many an R.E. lesson.

*

What kind of a world do you think information books show young readers? Is it threatened by disaster and division; does it demand new accountabilities and responsibilities? What provision do we make for the study of different versions of the lives of our European neighbours and our attitudes towards them?

Young people are appalled by pictures of calves huddled together in lorries, and by the suppression of the rights of individuals to protest about what they see as limitations on their freedom. Children should also know that they do not have to agree with everything they read and that what they are shown may need to be authenticated. If their experience persuades them that the opposite of what a book tells them might be the case, they should be encouraged to read *against* a text, or to write their own version of events or ideas. As Father Appleyard says in *Becoming a Reader*, children's reading of information books has all the qualities of their reading of quest tales. I think he is right, but I would add, only when the search seems worth while.

Reading information texts is not simply a cognitive process. Our current national curriculum in England aims to promote the moral development of children and society, but not everyone agrees about how this is to be done, or exactly what it implies. Consider these words of Phillida Salmon: 'If pupils are to contemplate the social problems in which they, like all of us, are implicated, they need first to articulate and then to begin to question how they understand their own everyday lives, their own cultural practices' (56).

Now we have to consider if there could be changes in ways of presenting information in book form to make sure that both reading and learning would, or at least might, be different. Meanwhile, as the result of this exercise, I am more persuaded than ever that 'issues' and moral attitudes and understandings are most effectively presented in novels and that collaborative focus on a task with an adult as well as a book is the key to children's intellectual growth.

ELEVEN

New Beginnings

The first steps in all learning tasks are the most significant. They shape our confidence, our views of our chances of success and give us some idea of the effort we are to make. Accomplishment is the result of persistence and practice fuelled by desire. Children are born as learners; their longing to *grasp* things, physically and mentally, is almost insatiable, especially in the early years. Unless they are socially restrained or hampered by too many failures, they are good learners.

Long before they see a book as a source of information, children have done a great deal of action research on the problems of sorting out their world. The role of books in early learning is recognizable when children's curiosity goes beyond controlling objects and people around them. Then they take their explorations a stage further for the sake of the kind of finding out we call knowing, even when it still looks like play. Books make most impact when they add to what experience offers, confirming and extending, in various book ways, what children are already aware of. Discovering books as a *place* for learning is a new beginning. But there is no single way for all children to learn this; they all have different learning preferences and styles.

Sorting out, in one form or another, is what information is good for: the kind of 'intellectual search' that Barbara Tizard describes in her study of four-year-olds. Questing intelligence, and the imagination we all possess but never fully exploit, link children's primitive grasp of the way things work with the kinds of adult inquiry that may radically change a common view of the world. Getting information from books is only the start; where children put it is every bit as important. What we call learning is the transformation of what is known by what is discovered. The most challenging topics for writers of learning books are those that deal with ordinary, everyday things that readers are invited to see differently. To provoke inquiry about water, air and fire seems straightforward, but the balance between the new and the taken-for-granted is always difficult, especially for beginners. Common assumptions are that, in books, the topic has to be 'scaled down', metaphoric descriptions kept at bay while presentations of the actual are to be foregrounded. Here is a snip from a fairly recent book simply called *Bread*. It is part of a science series for beginners.

Text	Picture
Everybody eats bread.	*Full face photo of a girl eating a sandwich*
Bread fills you up.	*Photo of a boy eating a French loaf*

Is this a good beginning? I wonder if young readers see this book information in relation to their own experience of one of the world's staple foods as the way they are expected to write about such things. Children could make their own books about bread much more interesting. Compared with what picture-book artists and authors do to draw children into books by offering them a richness of everyday detail that encourages looking and thinking (see Sarah Garland's books *Going Shopping* and *Doing the Washing*, read by children long before they come to school), this is pedagogic plodding that shuts out all imaginative recognition and speculation.

Children's moves into inquiry depend on the adults' willingness to accept the *proximal* nature of their understanding and their intellectual growth. Adults lend their minds out to the young not by simplifying what they know. Instead they engage the inquirer in the kind of looking and thinking where observation and language enhance and extend each other. Not all book learning begins with a book. Nevertheless, the books which awaken the readers' curiosity have a particular appeal, possibly because they are *not* like lessons. I suggest therefore that we need to revise, open up at least, our notions of what books for learning could be like. We need to rethink our common understandings of what constitutes a text that helps readers to learn not only the content and the register of the written language, but also the different *ways* of knowing.

My case is supported by the boundary-breaking series from Walker Books called 'Read and Wonder'. If we acknowledge the first freshness of early curiosity, the discovery of dew on spiders' webs, the clear archedness of bridges, changes of weather, movements of sea and wind, the fluidity of sand and water, that is, if we recollect initial curiosity and the first steps we still take to satisfy our longing to know, then we can approach this series of books as a new beginning in the early stages of book learning. The notion of reading and *wondering* indicates for me a re-vision of what makes learning exciting, attractive, successful; that is, reflection.

The books are all the same size, their only common feature. They are distinguishable by subject and presentation. Each book engages readers in a single reading act instead of the usual attempt to bind bits of the topic together. The innovative feature of the series, namely, its challenge to long-accepted notions of fiction and non-fiction, lets us consider whether or not we are prepared to go beyond the tyranny of the double-page spread and the inevitability of 'facts' in offering children books for learning. In 'Read and Wonder' books, two texts (in different types of setting) carry information, and both add to young readers' understanding of what reading can be like to match awakened interest in the topic. This is a recognition and a realization that book learning is intellectual and affective, at the same time.

Attracted by the visual display and the inviting nearness of the voice on the page, young learners see, and see through, the pictures and the words to the understanding generated by the clarity of the texts and the fine images. This new beginning in book learning moves away from the conventional ordering of subject matter. The inspiration and the generative models for 'Read and Wonder' come from modern picture books. The artist-writer-publisher collaborations in these productions have turned their best practices to books of information. To understand the series' potential adults have to see the subject matter in a context for which the categories of fiction and non-fiction are not appropriate.

I have written elsewhere about the poetic riches of *Think of an Eel* and mentioned *The Wheeling and Whirling around Book* and *A Piece of String is a Wonderful Thing* as brilliant presentations of ordinary actions and objects turned into exploitations of possibilities of thinking: problem solving, configurations and speculation about the nature of things. *Caterpillar Caterpillar* is Vivian French's account of her memory of watching caterpillar eggs become butterflies, over one childhood summer, with her grandfather. There is a kind of Proustian rightness in the matching and blending of this account with Charlotte Voake's exquisite page designs on just off-white paper. The effect is of pale sunlight through the leaves. The line drawings, delicately coloured and detailed, suggest sensitive looking and waiting. The whole, doubtless the result of editorial collaboration, offers an informative and aesthetic experience of reading. This conjoint showing and telling suggest that, where the eyes go, there go also delight and understanding. The opening endpaper sets the tone.

> It's impossible to say exactly when you'll find caterpillars. It depends on where you live, and what the weather's like, and all sorts of other things. The eggs I found were laid in May. They hatched out into caterpillars in June and changed their skins four times during the next month or so. The first three times I didn't see it happen, because they changed inside their tents. But I did see the fourth time . . .

The words face drawings of three different kinds of caterpillars, named and poised on the appropriate plant. The implied instructions are: look in spring; wait a month; see the skin change. The whole process is four months long. For the reader, the experience is calm, selective and, above all, attentive. Children learn so quickly that we are always tempted to let them run when their interest is caught and held. But it is not just by chance that gardening is the most prominent source of metaphors for children's development and growth over time. In this book, the watching child is warned what to be careful about and encouraged to look farther when the fresh clean caterpillar is later found 'like a little soft brown bag, hanging on the pea stick'. The judgement may be that this text is too girlish, too sentimental. It is certainly a change from the stern facticity of tractors and other technologies. But perhaps Darwin would have approved.

In several of these volumes we read about and see changes in nature, metamorphosis and mutability, the recurrent subjects of poetry. This is what children watch most on television, where the natural processes are speeded up. In reading, the imagination is actively transforming the inner speech of thought and the discernment of visual meanings into knowing by means of children's own metaphors.

We can't put the books in this series on a shelf marked 'non-fiction'. It is impossible to classify different kinds of writing by simple descriptions of their function, especially when they appear on the same pages, together with illustrations. Compare these books with other formulaic productions of topic material, then ask yourself if any standardization of photograph and paragraph makes book learning as attractive and approachable. These are books for beginners, but the features of the starting point are, in book learning as in any other kind, part of the children's awareness and anticipation of the task of book reading and learning. You may say that wondering is normal in the first stages of anything, and that, in later childhood, reading and knowing have to move to categorization and then to abstraction if scientific constructs are to be established. My answer is that unless real curiosity is sustained, speculative questioning dies.

In information texts we have seen many changes that keep them in line with advances in publishing and printing and updated subject matter. But the overall effect has remained the same, static even, delivering facts in a package with little reference to how reading is part of what is to be read. We need new beginnings for readers in search of ways of ordering the world by reading and thinking. 'Read and Wonder' seems to be a different kind of start, not least because the books suggest there is more to be known.

What, then, about information books for children who are just beginning to encounter 'subjects' in the textbooks of secondary school? This is a serious issue. Every teacher knows that adolescent reading is neither certain nor predictable. But it is better to overestimate the understanding of young people than to offer them cajoling texts that demand little intellectual effort. In this context, the British Natural History series produced by Whittet Books offers a different kind of learning experience. These are serious studies written by experts who are skilled communicators. They inform their readers with the lightness of touch, clarity and generosity of those who are entirely at ease with their specialist knowledge so that their focus is on the reader as *potential* expert. There are no false simplicities. Instead ample text room lets the writers and illustrators explain the features and life styles of badgers, bats, deer, eagles, whales, foxes, wildcats, puffins, otters, seals, rabbits, owls and other creatures, most of which the readers have already encountered in stories. The naturalists explain where their own interest comes from, share their experiences, and set the learner's growing knowledge in a wider domain of observation and scientific inquiry. Writing of this kind dignifies children's learning, not by being ponderous, but by taking it seriously.

Paul Chanin's *Otters* linked my recollection of *Tarka the Otter* and *The Ring of Bright Water* with more accurate current concerns about these elusive beasts. I have never seen an otter, but I'm sure I'd recognize one at once now that this expert has translated his direct observation into visual images for me. Too knowledgeable to be over-emphatic, Chanin says 'there is no reason why the animals should fit into neat categories we make for them, or even into the same categories everywhere they live', a frequent occurrence in lesser texts. In *Mice and Voles* by John Flowerdew I discovered just how disproportionate is the size of a mouse to its capacity for destruction, my interest overcoming my abhorrence.

Michael Chinery's *Spiders* springs a surprise on every page. The specialist discourse (including the use of Latin names) is as straightforward as conversation, a dialogue with any reader whose curiosity about spiders could be transformed into expertise. Observation elevates anecdote to evidence.

> I think I first became aware of the size of the spider population when I was at primary school. The footpath leading to the school was bounded by thick hedges which, on autumn mornings, were draped with sparkling, dew-laden webs. I don't think I ever counted them, but there were a lot and my friends and I amused ourselves on the way to school by collecting them on slender loops made from privet twigs. The sticky webs clung to the twigs and, with the dew trapped among the fine strands of silk, they eventually made a primitive sort of mirror—a bit like a soap film on a loop of wire. We used to have competitions to see who had the best one when we arrived at school. A really good one could be used to bounce a ping-pong ball, so we must have learned something about the elasticity of spider silk. (10-11)

This is a companionable book. The expert makes it possible for the reader to play the role of entomologist. Ordinary experiences, like brushing spiders into a dustpan when they collapse, are part of the learning process. Silk spinning, web weaving and venom pumping are meticulously explained and illustrated. Common assumptions about the fate of the male spider and the spider in the bath are exposed. Spider sex, unbelievably complex, is as compelling as any adventure story; the drawings are bound to astonish as well as to inform accurately. Readers can stop, look and return to the text, all the time feeling stretched and yet helped. The Latin names are part of the assumption that this is a stage in moving to categorization. The book is made to extend learning, the expert leading, the apprentice given responsibility for checking and speculating.

By hearing it read aloud, listeners remember what the author tells them, so the text is not beyond the competence of those who could read *What is a Bird?* Although there is more information in Chinery's text, there is also much more redundancy of the kind that reinforces remembering. The book demands stamina and perseverance but it need not be read all at once. Readers discover where the information is coming from and how to check it against their own experience. The result is not only learning but also a feeling of independence in learning.

There must be more books than I have found which assume that young readers are capable of sustained reading and learning when their interest has been awakened and engaged. A further problem remains: to ensure that teachers take the trouble to find and read such books.

Single outstanding texts do not, by themselves, build a course of planned topic learning in the way that current 'packs', in all their novelty, claim to do. Just as teachers feel steadied when they have recourse to reading schemes, so they have become accustomed to letting 'structured' books of information do the teaching of the topic content and organize the writing into a series of levels, each with its workbooks, cassettes and teachers' manuals. Many schools would like enough money to buy a curriculum based on weather, food and transport, all ready for 'delivery'. I have no doubt that, in some places, organized topic learning of this kind would be an advance, but I still believe it should be possible to demonstrate book learning that arises out of the fullness of knowing rather than from samples. We could begin with a series of case studies of how our most original and influential thinkers of the last twenty-five years acquired their specialist competences. Would they, do you think, give credit to the publishers of a non-fiction series for inspiring them?

There are signs of new beginnings. Although we are told that discoveries about information gathering and dissemination will make books an outmoded technology, the reality may be different. General concern about children's reading is fiercer than ever, and books are cheaper and handier for many learning purposes.

One thing stands out. When young people want to be involved in subjects that interest them, they do not turn first to the books they see in school and begin a deliberate, organized search. Instead they read what they find left lying around by their elders or in the newsagent's shop display, especially magazines about sport, cars, and computers where the latest thing is the most important. For their serious interests readers need books as well as 'part works' to help them to learn. James Britton wrote: 'The small boy whose chances of controlling an automobile are still at least a dozen years away may nevertheless treasure a great deal of knowledge about how automobiles work.' In twelve years young people are expected to learn much, and magazines will certainly cater for their desire for novelty. Books could confirm their knowing even more, if the writers, publishers and educators promoted reading, and wondering, more carefully, more seriously.

TWELVE

Critical Decisions

The only person who can really tell if a book of information has increased his or her understanding is the reader. Part of being able to read is knowing that if one book doesn't provide enough information, there are bound to be others. Good readers are constantly in search of the books that best fit the extent of their knowledge and their learning styles. Until they learn to browse, beginners look for the help and intervention of those who know which books will help them to learn. Teachers and librarians see this as part of their professional obligation, so they read book reviews and make lists.

Reviewing information books for children is almost as complicated as writing them. Judging the reviews compounds every difficulty. Whose views count? Whose judgement is to be relied upon? I believe that the best way to assess others' opinions of topic books is to write your own appraisal of a book you are attracted to. Then you will discover what you want a review to enlighten you about. So, before you read on, try composing a notice of about 200 words on a book of your choice to tell your implied readers what they will learn from it. You will also find that you have to answer the same questions that confront every author and every reviewer.

Who will be interested to read your opinion: the editor, the design team, the author, the publisher, subject specialists in secondary schools, generalists in primary classrooms, parents, makers of book lists? Who will be helped by what the text claims to teach; who will find it moderately easy, totally incomprehensible? Will your comments include references to topic structure, design and illustrations, layout, organization of materials, retrieval devices, assumptions about readers' prior knowledge? Will you be able to show how the contents are to link with other texts in the series, with the books in the bibliography? How accurate are the statements claimed to be facts? Have you been aware of gender bias? Is the book written with a multicultural audience in mind?

All these questions, and more, have been addressed in short review notices, by me and a host of others. It is never easy to be satisfied with the result. In the end, adjectives stand out as the significant words. Here is one reviewer's prompt question: 'What does this book tell the readers that they cannot possibly know they want to know before they get started to read it?' I think that, in the following review, below the surface of its short text, the writer has that question in mind.

Fakes and Forgeries Ian Graham, Evans (Science Spotlight series) 0 237 5194 7 £8.95

MIDDLE / SECONDARY

The processes and techniques involved in detecting fakes and forgeries are, in themselves, almost totally unexciting: chemical analysis, radio carbon dating, X- and other rays, spectrometry, refractometry and thermoluminescence arouse few passions on the page. So what is it that makes a book like this such compelling reading? It's the enormous range of things that people have thought it worthwhile to counterfeit—from Yeti scalps to the pound in your pocket—and the uneasy feeling that we may be the forger's next victim.

Here we have such an array, well displayed—for each in a succession of examples we find out how the dissembling was done and how it was detected. Piltdown Man, Hitler diaries, the Conan Doyle-seducing Cottingly Fairies, Tom Keating's 'Sexton Blakes' and assorted antiques, gems and coinage all get the treatment.

The appeal of the book is further widened by the inclusion of mysteries which may themselves attract fraudulent evidence, so Nessie, crop circles and UFOs get space too as we gradually learn about all the -ometries and -ologies involved, with sidelights on security.

Less of a science book than its series title suggests, this is a competently assembled list of famous fakes with a serviceably informative text capable of creating genuine interest. TP

This review commends itself not simply for its responsible summary of the book's contents and a short clear judgement with adjectival and adverbial qualifications. It also demonstrates how the book *creates* 'genuine interest', implying as it does so that the application of scientific discovery begins off the set subject curriculum with the question: why do people fake things? The scientific organization of the knowledge offered to the reader comes as a consequence of awakening genuine curiosity.

Who, then, will read this review? The readers of *Books for Keeps*, all those who have discovered this journal as a reliable source of information over a wide range of books for the young, will be intrigued. They may not buy the book or even think of it again if it does not fall within their remit as providers. Thus the reviewing discourse itself becomes a set of conventions, a way to understand what is being done.

Not the only way, of course. In that same issue Ted Percy, who wrote the review above, is the author of an article about gardening books for children. He includes thirty-three titles, beginning like this:

What is it, after all, that makes gardening so utterly worth doing? I've been trying to answer this question for years now and still don't really know, but I think the important thing is the stewardship of soil—your own soil—however much or little.

This is why the whole drama of *The Secret Garden* hinges on that part of the story where, surprising herself by the directness of her question, Mary asks Mr Craven 'might I have a bit of earth?' When the bewildered benefactor asks why, Mary falters 'to plant seeds in—to make things grow—to see them come alive'. Confused but convinced, Craven invites her to take whatever earth she wants, then in the next chapter she finds Colin and the story—uncertain in its progress to this point— climbs hand over green-fingered hand to feature film status.

The article length lets the reviewer lay out the foundation of his conviction, extended in the next paragraph, that it's the 'bit of earth that matters'. He continues:

A perennial delight has been Pat Hutchins's *Titch*, where the littlest member of a family trio, relegated always to the least impressive roles, plants a 'tiny seed . . . and it grew and it grew and it grew' and Titch's self-esteem grows with it. Then, six years ago, Beverley and Nick Birch produced *Our Hidden Garden*. Here a happy multicultural crowd enjoys enormous enrichment of life in the garden that is both centre and surroundings for their outwardly ordinary inner London infants' school. The pleasure and purpose that the garden brings to its school is a joy to see and I only hope that the garden still survives—in the current educational climate it's needed more than ever. A particular private joy motivates Jan Mark's *This Bowl of Earth*. By the back door, warmed by the heating vent and damped by the drain, the bowl is a perfect nursery for cuttings to grow until they are ready for planting in the author's garden of trees. Here we get narrative and information in a harmonious real-life mix and, as in real life, some of the cuttings take and some don't. But the bowl goes on—an absorbing and utterly achievable garden in its own right as the author's gentle words explain how so lowly a thing can be so special.

Here is a reviewer showing that for him the fact-fiction separation doesn't exist in books for the young. Books are embedded in each other. Mary and Titch are gardeners. The reader-reviewer also includes his desires for and experience of gardens as part of his judgement of the books when he says of *My First Garden Book*: 'I wish I knew where they found that brand new miniature watering can—it's a beauty.'

What shines out from good criticism and judgement of information books is a distinctive kind of *connoisseurship*, a linking of knowledge and appreciation. It is possible, but difficult, to convey this distinctive quality in a short reviewing space. The virtue is, of itself, expansive. Reading the enthusiasm of an expert is like listening to someone who really knows a subject well treating you as an insider, a member of the guild, a sharer in the mysteries, even if you have never considered the topic before. When I look back, I know that the things which have concerned me most come from books that offered me this kind of encounter. They have made knowing seem within my grasp because the writer wants to bring it there. So if I say that I judge best the reviews written by those who convey their enthusiasm, I am taking a short cut in describing what is, in reading, a deep kind of joy.

It is easy to find fault with books designed for school learning. The author is inexact, out of date, says the subject expert. The design is muddled, aesthetically poor, says the prize-winning illustrator. It's too easy, too difficult, too boring, says the inexperienced reader. Too expensive, is the librarian's opinion. It doesn't fit the curriculum, has no index, isn't multicultural enough, are the views of the inspectors. They'd rather watch TV, say the parents. The cynics hardly glance and say, it's all part of publicity.

I think we are still trying to come to terms with different kinds of readers and the world-wide range of their interests. Reviewers are readers whose claim is that they can read on behalf of others, but that assertion can never be true if they are only showing off how well they themselves can read, or what they know that the writers of the books do not.

Despite this ziggurat of complaints, information books have their supporters, those who want to show that informed comment can make a difference. But to make reviews matter, reviewers have to build up a continuous connoisseurship which is different from writing occasional short notices, important though these are. To gather strength and influence in the realm of so-called 'nonliterary' texts, as it has with stories and poems, reviewing needs to become sustained writing about books and learning. Also, while most adults who are interested in children's literature have now discovered that there is nothing childish about children's fiction, the same is not true about books of information for use in school. Built into most topic books is the message: this is for young people who are still learning to read this kind of text. Not surprisingly, therefore, the most perceptive commentators have close contacts with readers as learners. But they also retain their adult view of how success in understanding the topic can be brought about and have their own ideas of how the difficulties in providing suitable texts can be surmounted.

This is true of Bobbie Neate, for example. In *Finding out about finding out* she says, with reason, that information books are 'the Cinderella of texts'. The principal shortcomings are that the books are too varied in function, readability, depth of topic, register, specialist language and the commitment of authors, and that children have no consistent group of texts from which to learn the skills of informative reading. 'Young children are probably the last group of readers who should be given such a wide variety of texts. They need a model from which to learn and with which to become familiar.' Neate's solution is to have a 'collaborative team of reading experts working together with publishers' to ensure that the 'fundamental aim of children's books should be to create a dialogue between writer and reader'.

I doubt it. No group of experts, however collaborative, can be guaranteed to produce a set of texts which teach book learning as a process, and, at the same time, are interesting across a wide range of subject matters. There is no single, effective way to design information books which will suit the *learning* styles of all readers. Quite the reverse. The variety Neate bewails is exactly what makes children's picture books so effective in displaying what reading can be like. The texts of the 'Read and Wonder' series, all different, arise out of the diversity of ways of learning and knowing. No book formula could encompass their invitation to speculative curiosity. Neate believes that children should be encouraged to ask: 'Do I enjoy this book? Can I learn from it? Can I find the answers to my questions?' Agreed. But, 'consistent' texts would be constrictive and normative in ways that could add to children's reading and learning problems the whole business of 'getting it right'. One sure lesson from book learning we all know: the same information can be presented in different *versions* and in different contexts, hence the need for careful reviewing.

Connoisseurship, like book learning itself, takes many forms. Although most information books are the result of editorial teamwork, what the readers reproduce, in exams or other kinds of schoolwork, comes closest to the writing they read in print. It isn't easy to quote pictures, although these are often more important sources of information and some readers are skilled in taking meaning from these. But it is the reproduction of the discourse, the accepted way of writing about a subject, that is usually taken to be the best indicator of a learner's grasp of the topic or subject 'matter'.

Librarians have always encouraged the view that, as sources of information, two books are better than one. The connoisseurship of specialist librarians, like Peggy Heeks and Keith Barker, expresses itself in the kind of vigilance that keeps booklists up-to-date. Reviewing as book selection seems straightforward only to those who take the results of others' care for granted. From her influential position of reviews editor of nonfiction in *Books for Keeps*, Eleanor von Schweinitz confronts the complex issues of reviewing by means of selected examples which display the strengths and weaknesses of the books being considered. Her articles are long enough and her illustrations particular enough to make good general points clearly. Strictures fall on books which 'lack any focus'. 'A successful book will explain, expand, illustrate and reinforce key ideas, often through the close interaction of text and illustration.' Emphasizing, importantly, that pictures don't *explain* a subject, she is scathing about those which 'present difficult concepts in a highly condensed form and in total isolation'. She looks for 'a well-integrated structure', 'structural coherence' and a 'readable text'. She denounces packagers who are 'frequently in danger of sacrificing coherence and intelligibility to eyecatching page design.'

In reviews the knowledge base of the writer has to be matched, in part at least, by that of the adult reader. The reviewer has to know whether or not the details the writer chooses are apposite to the view of the subject matter designed for a growing reader and not only the facts themselves but also the implications the writer wants to convey. This may be more straightforward for the reader in discussions of the composition of water than in accounts of the history of South Africa. If the text is for very young readers, what counts as essential knowing is always the most difficult thing to determine. Our current worries about the education of our children, and about our own, stem from the fact that we are not sure what counts as 'common' knowledge. Reviewers are also bound to discover whether or not the book shows how the information was acquired and how it can be best understood. These references are not often included in shorter books, and only sometimes in longer ones.

'A good information book', says Jennifer Wilson, 'is a model for children's learning.' Her judgement is that children are short-changed by the book team's belief that the purpose of information books for children is to simplify the world. Short length and restricted vocabulary 'rob a topic of its intrinsic interest'. Some of the children's prior understandings turn out to be 'myths . . . which must be displaced before knowledge will gain a foothold'. The teacher's responsibility is not simply to see that all children have books, but to make sure that the next stage of learning will have a starting point.

Across the range of all school learning we have no clear idea of what information books *could* be like. Apart from those whose work we have glimpsed here, reviewers tend to take the books as they are. Some look for possibilities of 'skimming and scanning', although these processes are bound to be different in each discourse kind. Reviews rarely offer a comment on the 'hidden conjectural features': that is, what the book makers assume all children know, and what they are expected to learn by reading beyond what the words actually say to what they mean or imply.

If information books for the young are transitory stuff, demanding more in the writing and reading than reviews ever display, complicated by generalizations and exceptions as well as a recurrent sense of the banality, insufficiency and repetitiousness of the books themselves, why are they not simply regarded as ephemeral as magazines? Why do we persist in believing, as I certainly do, that reviewing is important?

In the early 1980s the Head of the Bulgarian children's book agency asked me this question and others. How could there be more than one valid judgement of the worth of a book to be read by children? Surely the way to avoid individual prejudice was to appoint a selection committee, or a panel of acknowledged writers? This is not an uncommon practice even outside the former Soviet bloc. In the United States, locally recommended and selected reading schemes make their publishers rich. French schools use specially written course books; Fernand Braudel, the pre-eminent historian of civilization, wrote one. In England teachers are now being cajoled away from their traditional freedom to choose the books they believe to be most suitable for the children they teach and to accept 'suggestions' for primary school reading and secondary school study.

With so many books in print, and so few of them locally available or seen outside catalogues, it is not surprising that a formal list of books for use in school seems desirable to many, especially teachers who find choosing 'suitable' books time-consuming or frustrating as the result of their inexperience in reading them. But *all* official selections come with a hidden curriculum of approved ideas, and a degree of censorship of books deliberately not chosen. If reviews were more explicit, varied and written by respected critics, teachers and librarians would be helped to resist some of the poor choices made by anonymous list-makers.

Here are some ideas still to be worked on.

First, there is no check-list of desirable qualities or necessary features which all reviewers can use in looking for books that are 'suitable'.

Next, some young readers are already experts in the subjects that interest them. They need adult books to dip into, to move

113

around in, to exert their knowing against. Reviewers are not always the best readers to judge what kinds of books are 'difficult', although they almost invariably do.

Likewise, beginners shouldn't be confined to the simple naming of objects in pictures. They too need more.

But if selected lists are to be part of the judgement of books for school use, then the selectors should be known and be made publicly responsible for their choices. Books of information have to be checked for straightforward mistakes. Bias and partial viewpoints will persist, so in the libraries children use there should be more than one book on a topic across a fairly wide age range. Librarians know the nature of reviews from the contexts in which they appear. They look to a journal like *The School Librarian* to examine different kinds of *documentation*, the word that includes all kinds of versions of the world on paper designed for study use. Even so, the dearth of insight and skilled writing in utilitarian texts is daunting.

Whenever I began to research a topic for this exercise, I found too many books to consider in detail, but I felt I had to read most of them in order to modify my prejudices. Some of them went out of print. Others were out-of-date. My notes showed that I found more to complain about than to praise, which was not part of my intention but difficult to avoid. Teachers seemed to buy books that had been well reviewed only after they had been remaindered. In their selection of titles from the now fast-diminishing library services, they were depending on the recommendations of colleagues or the enthusiasms of some pupils, which meant that the range of sources was becoming narrower. In many cases, adults did not read the texts but simply passed them over to the pupils, who made of them what they could. Courses on book learning ceased to be part of the continuing education of teachers.

However, the tide is slowly turning. Teachers and librarians can no longer simply order sets of books from catalogues. Now they have to make critical decisions when they choose learning materials, including the expensive software designed to match the new technologies, CD-ROM in particular. As the result of a government initiative in subsidizing machines, the disks bring the contents of a well-stocked library within the sightlines of children in many primary schools. In respect of the technology, pupils are often more skilled, and more confident, than their teachers.

Important considerations are emerging. With the historical prescience of their trade, publishers are transferring book materials to computerized formats and, in some cases, beginning to rethink how books and information technology could complement each other. Where children were thought to need help with study skills to read printed information texts, they now demonstrate how they transfer their enthusiasm for computer games and their skill in playing them to exploring the storage potential of multimedia nonlinear texts. In addition, their everyday experience of discussing and reviewing TV programmes makes them unself-conscious critics of what they find on disks. If their disk search is unsatisfactory, they turn, willingly, to the books they once believed were difficult to read. Already there is evidence that teachers respond to learners' eager confidence in this new literacy by demonstrating the constructedness of texts, the connectedness of different kinds of information and how these processes relate to growth in conceptual understanding. This is not all happening everywhere at once, but teachers have begun to see the potential of book learning in a new light and to demand more challenging texts.

At the time when young people want to know more about the world, they look to television for revelations about it, which is why they see possibilities in multimedia texts. In the current conditions of most schools, they discover the imaginative breadth of learning from their best teachers, especially those who lend them books, rather than from the specified contents of the curriculum. The question most young teenage learners try to frame is, why is the world thus and not otherwise? But in too many lessons they encounter the world in bits, with no vision of the long perspective that is the bonus of learning to reflect, to think about thinking. Contrast the 'Tudors and Stuarts' in the class discussion of seven-year-olds with the vivacity of their playground conversations about the events of their lives and the experiences they bump into. When we listen to young people talking about the books they read to learn, we discover they have quite distinctive views about them. A nine-year-old said she liked the book *Explorations and Encounters* because it is 'all dark colours and there are no light colours'. Another pupil in the same class said about *Vikings* that he 'needed more about Vikings and less about craft'. A boy who liked *Knights in Armour* said, 'You see people ready for their heads chopped off.'

What seems to make learning memorable is not the generality of things or situations, nor the understanding of categories of experience. Instead, it is the light shed on a topic by the anomalous cases, the aberrant details, the singular instances all fraught with the possibilities of becoming either a good story or a speculative hypothesis, or both. Long after the exact dates are forgotten, the grisly particulars of the Black Death or the plague and the great fire of London echo in the memory as examples of human catastrophe. On a smaller scale Margaret Mallett showed her pupils pictures of squirrels during their study of them. The image most closely examined showed a squirrel with mange.

CODA

This exercise in thinking about book learning began when my explorations of the nature of contemporary literacy showed that the increased production of printed materials in the so-called information explosion, together with the extensions of technocratic communication systems powered by 'market forces', would probably change the entire social context of literate behaviours. I wondered what reading to learn would be like, both in the world and in school, if books were no longer the primary means of learning from texts. Also, there seemed to be too little evidence of how children learned to read to learn, as distinct from how teachers were encouraged to teach them to do it. This seemed strange, given that at least half of the books published for children are intended to inform them directly.

Here are my last examples. In the usual primary school library, or even for use in a class, it is difficult to keep intact *The Most Amazing Pop-Up Science Book*. It's a book for two readers to explore together, or one alone. (A sharing adult should not take it over.) Inside, the pages are three-dimensional models, lying flat, of a record player with a stylus, a compass, a microscope, a camera obscura, a sundial, a kaleidoscope and a periscope. When it is unfolded, the disc on the record player can be made to emit Edison's first recorded words. The other instruments invite the reader to experiment with ways of looking and seeing. My eight-year-old partner was confident that the book engineering would work, so he spent an hour experimenting with the pop-ups, successfully except for the sundial. The microscope produced the most dramatic transformations. The example in the book was a bed-mite magnified 340 times. The notion that a million such creatures, all eyes and teeth, roamed in every mattress, led us to a discussion of other things that might be beyond the 'naked eye'. In reading the printed text my partner picked out the words that intrigued him ('light year'), and seemed to ignore others that were unfamiliar. Following clues from what he had already heard about, he guessed 'retinal image' in relation to the camera because 'we did the eye in school'. His ordinary seeing became a topic for comment as he realized that three of the instruments extended it.

In our talk we made some little heaps of understandings and sorted out some extra examples. (My bifocal glasses came into play.) There was no need for me to close down the topic, as is often the case in school when there is something next on the timetable. I also managed to restrain myself from ladling out more information than the book offered unless the given explanation was too compressed. (Too much information is actually worse than too little.) My young reader talked about what he had seen before he put my remarks alongside his. He also needed more explicit explanations of how the examples fitted the generalizations. These things will change over time. No topic is ever finished, only recursively re-examined. Meanwhile, we were exploring a small part of the world of science, using talk to bring us to a collaborative focus. Talk is the key to the growth of children's understanding. What I learned was that, in not much more than an hour, my young companion traversed ideas that had emerged over centuries of patient human observation and trial-and-error learning by scholars and scientists who persisted because they saw the importance of turning information into understanding and understanding into knowledge.

Cognitive scientists have different names for the stages of children's thinking. I borrow a term from my friend and colleague Peter Medway to describe the kind of learning I was trying to support. He calls it *predisciplinary*. Young learners have 'sets of awareness' before they make generalizations or propositions. From a given example they imagine others. The conversations they engage in with their good teachers and more experienced friends continue as dialogues in the head.

Finally, there is The Topic: a centre of interest which children explore intensively by reading, writing and talking about it, then offering their 'findings' to their classmates by presenting them in the form of collaborative writing. (Margaret Mallett's book has an extended example.) On a number of occasions I have analysed and written about what happens in relation to this enterprise, not only in classrooms but more particularly when the topic is a holiday task. As I helped small groups of pupils I discovered some of their perplexities as well as their pleasures in book learning. For example, they always tried to find out 'how much does she want?' or 'how long does it have to be?' in order to discern the importance of the work in terms of the teacher's marks or appraisal. So my concern was to engage them with an aspect of the topic they would recognize as worth some effort beyond the due performance of what was expected of them, then the finding-out would be more than what James Britton called a 'dummy run', a kind of pretending to discover. Many books on 'doing a topic' tell young learners to state at the start what they want to find out. The fact is, they can't know what this is until they have sidled up to a subject with a whole list of questions. There are many ways into a topic, but they all involve reading and talking in the mode of a quest, not for something startling or new but to make the learning experience an authentic one. When time presses, and it nearly always does, I find it helpful to settle first the presentational format for the results and how much writing there is time for, which means when to stop talking and put the significant ideas and examples together, often in narrative.

You have only my word for it, but the more I work with beginners on topic search and 'writing up', the more I am struck by the similarity between their rituals and those of my most advanced research students. Discovering begins with the learner's understanding of the topic so far, and the advances come from reading around it, making the new understandings modify, then extend the existing ones. The best thing I do as a research assistant in a school setting is to collect as many books as possible for the learners to browse through, while leaving them some time for library searches on their own. Browsing is a great skill in book learning; it needs only demonstration to be successfully accomplished. I have never been better rewarded than when I helped some boys who were sorting out the details of the American War of Independence. They discovered that they could read the actual words of those who had been engaged in the conflict, on both sides, because they were all in English. Most of their sources were adult books, which made the enterprise seem important, but when they wanted to know what a 'minuteman' was, they had *Sam the Minuteman,* an American book for beginning readers that explained it exactly.

Believing as I do that learning is a process of coming-to-know, I find it difficult to understand why the collaboration of adults and children is regarded as inappropriate in the contexts of school assessment. Those who are persuaded that knowledge is directly transmitted from a book, a lesson or a lecture, object to parents helping children with 'course work' on the grounds that this is a kind of cheating, and say that some children would be at a greater advantage than others. Most teachers I know would spot a parental paragraph a mile off and take appropriate tactful action. They also know that the education system is unfair in many other respects.

As I write this, reading to learn extends beyond books and other linear texts in print. My hope is that the means of diffusion of information will not overwhelm what is important for people to know. As a critical literacy, book learning has definite advantages. The reader sees entirely what the text is, and what there is to be read, and believes that whoever wrote it is prepared to be responsible for its contents. As yet, this is not the case with computerized materials. Likewise we are bound to see that the ideas behind many information texts, across a number of modes, are predominantly male in the conception and presentation of topics and examples. Stephen Biesty's work is a case in point, but there are many others who lack his sophistication and skill. One sentence in eighteen pages, 'Ladies drive tractors too', hardly redresses the gender balance. Worst of all is the condescending treatment of topics such as women's suffrage in books of social history.

In discussing books designed to add information to children's learning it is difficult, certainly much more difficult than with fiction for young people, to keep readers in mind. This is a problem for writers and design teams. But from time to time we catch glimpses of writers who want to share their accumulated understanding with their readers, and who offer them learning in a different sense by 'lending their minds out'. Then a reader begins to see that coming to understand the world is a single enterprise, with many books, many different kinds of texts and different versions, which no single account can encompass.

119

References

Sue Adler, 'Versions of Reality', *Language Matters*, journal of the Centre for Language in Primary Education, no. 2, 1990

Janet & Allan Ahlberg, *The Baby's Catalogue*, Kestrel, 1982

Mitsumasa Anno, *The Earth is a Sundial*, Bodley Head, 1986

J.A. Appleyard, *Becoming a Reader: The Experience of Fiction from Childhood to Adulthood*, Cambridge University Press, 1990

Julie Asquith, 'Dissecting Daffodils', *Language Matters*, journal of the Centre for Language in Primary Education, no. 2, 1990

W.H. Auden, 'Freedom and Necessity in Poetry: My Lead Mine', reprinted from 'The Place of Value in a World of Facts', *Nobel Symposium* 14, eds. A. Tiselius & S. Nilsson, Almqvist & Wiksell, 1970, in *Play: its role in development and evolution*, eds. J.S. Bruner, A. Jolly & K. Sylva, Penguin Books, 1976

Myra Barrs, 'Maps of Play', *Language and Literacy in the Primary School*, eds. Margaret Meek & Colin Mills, Falmer Press, 1988

Gregory Bateson, *Mind and Nature, a necessary unity*, Wildwood House, 1979

David Bernie, *Eyewitness Guide: Birds*, Dorling Kindersley, 1992

Stephen Biesty, *Incredible Cross-Sections*, text by Richard Platt, Dorling Kindersley, 1992

Books for Keeps, 6 Brightfield Road, Lee, London SE12 8QF

James Britton, *Language and Learning*, Penguin Books, 1992

Peter Brown, with the Royal Geographical Society, *Brunei Rainforest Adventure*, BBC Books, 1993

Anthony Browne, *Gorilla*, Julia MacRae, 1992

Jerome Bruner, *Actual Minds, Possible Worlds*, Harvard University Press, 1986

Karen Bryant-Mole, *Bullying* (What's Happening? series), Wayland, 1992

Bullock Report, *A Language for Life*, HMSO, 1975

David Bygott, *Black and British*, Oxford University Press, 1992

Centre for Language in Primary Education, Webber Row, London SE1 8QW

J. Chall, *Learning to Read: The Great Debate*, McGraw-Hill, 1967; 1983

Aidan Chambers, *The Present Takers*, Bodley Head, 1983

Paul Chanin, *Otters*, illustrated by Guy Troughton, Whittet Books, 1993

Michael Chinery, *Spiders*, illustrated by Sophie Allington, Whittet Books, 1993

Babette Cole, *Mummy Laid an Egg*, Jonathan Cape, 1994

John Amos Comenius, *Orbis Sensualium Pictus*, 1658. Facsimile of the London edition, 1672, Sydney University Press, 1967

Creating a Community of Readers, video directed by Jennifer Murray, University of Brighton, 1993

Robert Cumming, *Just Look . . .: A Book about Paintings*, Kestrel, 1979

Charles Darwin, *The Autobiography of Charles Darwin 1809-1882, with original omissions restored*, edited with Appendix and Notes by his grand-daughter, Nora Barlow, Collins, 1958

Florence Davies, *Books in the School Curriculum*, a Report from the National Book League, Publishers' Association, 1986

Roddy Doyle, *Paddy Clarke Ha Ha Ha*, Secker & Warburg, 1993

Umberto Eco, *The Name of the Rose*, Secker & Warburg, 1983

Umberto Eco, *Reflections on 'The Name of the Rose'*, Secker & Warburg, 1985

Eyewitness, A Universal Language for Learning, Dorling Kindersley, 1983

John Flowerdew, *Mice and Voles*, illustrated by Steven Kirk, Whittet Books, 1993

Michael Foreman, *Dinosaurs and All That Rubbish*, Hamish Hamilton, 1972

Carol Fox, *At the Very Edge of the Forest: The Influence of Literature on Storytelling by Children*, Cassell, 1993. (The main evidence for this book comes from Josh Hook's oral narratives, transcripts of some of which are reproduced here.)

Anne Frank, *The Diary of Anne Frank*, Pan, 1954

Vivian French, *Caterpillar Caterpillar* (Read and Wonder series), illustrated by Charlotte Voake, Walker Books, 1993

Sarah Garland, *Doing the Washing*, Bodley Head, 1983

Sarah Garland, *Going Shopping*, Bodley Head, 1982

Gwen Gawith, *Library Alive! promoting reading and research in the school library*, A. & C. Black, 1987

David & Jane Glover, *Bread*, Ginn Science Information Book, Level 1, Ginn, 1991

William Golding, *The Spire*, Faber, 1964

Angela Grunsell, *Let's Talk about Racism*, Franklin Watts, 1990

The Guinness Book of Records, Guinness Company, annual

George Hart, *Eyewitness Guide to Ancient Egypt*, Dorling Kindersley, 1990

Judy Hindley, *A Piece of String is a Wonderful Thing* (Read and Wonder series), illustrated by Margaret Chamberlain, Walker Books, 1993

Judy Hindley, *The Wheeling and Whirling around Book* (Read and Wonder series), Walker Books, 1994

Shirley Hughes, *Alfie Gets in First*, Bodley Head, 1981

Robert Hull, *The Language Gap: How classroom dialogue fails*, Methuen, 1985

Eric L. Huntley, *Two Lives: Florence Nightingale and Mary Seacole*, Bogle L'Ouverture Press, 1993

Melissa Kim, *The Blue Whale*, illustrated by Shirley Felts, Hutchinson, 1994

David Lambert, *The Ultimate Dinosaur Book*, Dorling Kindersley, 1993

Ursula Le Guin, 'It Was a Dark and Stormy Night; or, Why Are We Huddling about the Campfire?', *On Narrative*, ed. W.J.T. Mitchell, University of Chicago Press, 1981

Claire Llewellyn, *My First Book of Time*, Dorling Kindersley, 1992

Eric Lunzer & Keith Gardner, eds., *The Effective Use of Reading*, Schools Council, Heinemann, 1979

Eric Lunzer & Keith Gardner, eds., *Learning from the Written Word*, Oliver & Boyd, 1984

Jerome J. McGann, *The Textual Condition*, Princeton Paperbacks, 1991

David Macaulay, *Castle*, Collins, 1977

David Macaulay, *Cathedral*, Collins, 1974

David Macaulay, *City*, Collins, 1975

David Macaulay, *Pyramid*, Collins, 1975

David Macaulay, with Neil Ardley, *The Way Things Work*, Dorling Kindersley, 1988

Margaret Mallett, *Making Facts Matter: Reading Non-Fiction 5-11*, Paul Chapman, 1992

William Mayne, *Cathedral Wednesday*, Oxford University Press, 1960

Peter Medway, *Finding a Language: Autonomy and Learning in School*, Writers & Readers Publishing Cooperative, 1980

Margaret Meek. See Liz Thomson & Margaret Meek.

Margaret Meek, 'The critical challenge of the world in books for children', in *Celebrating 'Children's Literature in Education'*, edited by Geoff Fox, Hodder & Stoughton, 1995

Margaret Meek, 'What is a horse?', *The School Librarian*, vol. 25 no. 1, March 1977

Susan Meridith, *What's Inside You?* (Starting Point Science), illustrated by Kuo Kang Chen, Colin King & Peter Wingham, Usborne, 1991

Jonathan Miller, *The Facts of Life*, illustrated by David Pelham, Jonathan Cape, 1984/1995

Jonathan Miller, *The Human Body*, illustrated by David Pelham, Jonathan Cape, 1983/1995

Hilary Minns, unpublished thesis on the teaching of reading, quoting Richard Whateley's *The Second Book of Lessons*, published in Ireland in the nineteenth century and found in a Derbyshire workhouse

James Moffett, *Teaching the Universe of Discourse*, Houghton Mifflin, 1968

Patrick Moore, *The Starry Sky*, Riverswift, 1994

Bobbie Neate, *Finding out about finding out: a practical guide to children's information books*, Hodder & Stoughton, in association with the United Kingdom Reading Association, 1992

David Olson, 'On the Language and Authority of Textbooks', *Language, Authority and Criticism: Readings in the School Textbook*, eds., Suzanne de Castell, Allan Luke & Carmen Luke, Falmer Press, 1989

George Ordish, *The Great Wine Blight*, Dent, 1972; foreword by Jancis Robinson, Sidgwick & Jackson, 1986

Oxford Children's Dictionary, Oxford University Press, 1976, 3rd edition 1993

Oxford Senior Dictionary, Oxford University Press, 1982

Christine Pappas, 'Exploring the Global Structure of Children's Information Books', paper presented to the Annual Meeting of the National Reading Conference, Austin, Texas, 1986

Steve Parker, *Darwin and Evolution* (Science Discoveries), Belitha Press, 1992

Ted Percy, review of *Fakes and Forgeries*, *Books for Keeps*, no. 85, March 1994

Ted Percy, 'A Bit of Earth', *Books for Keeps*, no. 85, March 1994

Jean Piaget, *The Moral Judgment of the Child*, Routledge & Kegan Paul, 1932

Reading on Screen: Exploring Issues for Reading with CD-ROM, London Borough of Redbridge CD-ROM Group. Paper presented at NCET Colloquium for English and IT, February 1996, Birmingham

Brian Rosen, private letter to Myra Barrs about narrative in science

Dr Pete Rowan, *The Amazing Voyage of the Cucumber Sandwich: A story in three parts set in the human body*, illustrated by Polly Noakes, Jonathan Cape, 1991

Dr Pete Rowan, *Some Body!*, illustrated by John Temperton, Riverswift, 1994

Phillida Salmon, *Psychology in the Classroom: The Reconstruction of Teachers and Learners*, Cassell, 1995

Sheila Sancha, *Walter Dragun's Town*, Collins, 1987

Pete Saunders, *What do you know about bullying?*, Franklin Watts, 1993

Pam Schweitzer, et al., eds., *Goodnight Children, Everywhere*, Age Exchange Theatre Trust, 1990

School Librarian, School Library Association, Liden Library, Barrington Close, Liden, Swindon SN3 6HF

David Scott, 'Mental Imagery and the Process of Visualisation in Map Reading', New Series Discussion Paper no. 16, London School of Economics, Department of Geography, 1986

Frank Smith, *to think*, Teachers College Press, Columbia University, 1990

Robert Snedden, *What is a Bird?*, Belitha Press, 1992

Herbert Spencer, *Education, Intellectual, Moral and Physical*, Osnabrück: Otto Zeller, 1861

Rosemary Sutcliff, *The Eagle of the Ninth*, Oxford University Press, 1954

Rosemary Sutcliff, *The Lantern Bearers*, Oxford University Press, 1959

Liz Thomson & Margaret Meek, *Developing Resource-Based Learning: One School's Approach*, Schools Curriculum Development Committee, Longman, 1988

Barbara Tizard & Martin Hughes, *Young Children Learning: Talking and Thinking at Home and at School*, Fontana, 1984

Sue Townsend, *The Secret Diary of Adrian Mole aged 13¾*, Methuen, 1982

Barbara Tuchman, *A Distant Mirror: the calamitous 14th century*, Penguin, 1979

Lynn Underwood, *Religions of the World* (Information Library), Belitha Press, 1991

Eleanor von Schweinitz, 'Facing the Facts', *Books for Keeps*, no. 55, March 1989

L.S. Vygotsky, *Mind in Society*, Harvard University Press, 1978

Karen Wallace, *Think of an Eel* (Read and Wonder series), illustrated by Mike Bostock, Walker Books, 1993

Brenda Walpole, *Time* (Millipedes series), A. & C. Black, 1992

Hayden White, 'The value of narrativity in the representation of reality', *On Narrative*, ed. W.J.T. Mitchell, University of Chicago Press, 1981

Barbara Willard, Mantlemass novels, Longman/Kestrel, 1970-80

Raymond Williams, *The Country and the City*, Paladin, 1973

Jennifer Wilson, 'Choosing Information Books', *Signal* 39, September 1982

David Wray, 'Teaching Information Skills in the Primary School', unpublished paper, much of it contained in *Teaching Information Skills Through Project Work*, Hodder & Stoughton, 1985

David Wray, with Maureen Lewis, 'Primary Children's Use of Information Books', *Reading*, vol. 26 (3), 1992

Jay Young, *The Most Amazing Pop-Up Science Book: A Three-Dimensional Exploration*, Watts, 1994

Index